Stop Trying So Hard To Sleep

Easy 10-Minute CBT-I Habits to Ease Anxiety & Insomnia to Sleep Better

Julia Bennett

Twenty Squares Publishing

Contents

Introduction

It's 11:30 PM. You are lying in bed, exhausted from a long day. You should be asleep by now, but instead you are wide awake, mind racing, body tense, watching the minutes tick by.

You calculate how many hours of sleep you will get if you fall asleep right now. Then you recalculate as another fifteen minutes pass.

You have tried the usual things, from meditation apps, sleep trackers, expensive supplements, new pillows, white noise, to earlier nights and stricter routines. Some things may have helped a little. Nothing has really solved it. And the harder you try to sleep, the more elusive sleep seems to become.

If this sounds familiar, you are not alone. Around one in three adults struggles with insomnia symptoms, and many more go through periods when sleep becomes difficult. Poor sleep can affect everything: energy, mood, relationships, work, confidence and health. Yet despite how common it is, most people are left piecing together advice from articles, apps, product claims and well-meaning tips that do not always fit real life.

Your nights may be disrupted by racing thoughts, physical tension, early waking, pain, stress, hormones, medication, a snoring partner, or simply the fear of another bad night. You may not know exactly why your sleep has changed. That is all right. You do not need to solve everything at once.

Overthinking sleep is one of the most common ways insomnia keeps itself going. The more you focus on how tired you will feel tomorrow, the harder it can be to drift off tonight. This has a name, and it's called sleep anxiety and it's one of the reasons that CBT-I, or Cognitive Behavioral Therapy for Insomnia, was developed.

CBT-I is one of the best-supported long-term approaches for chronic insomnia, and it does not rely on gadgets, supplements or trying to force sleep into submission.

This book adapts CBT-I principles into simple, daily habits you can start using right away. You will learn how to rebuild trust in your body, reframe anxious thoughts, and use practical tools to support your sleep system without chasing perfection.

Sleep problems are rarely neat. One person lies awake because her mind will not stop. Another falls asleep quickly, then wakes at 3 AM with a racing heart. Someone else sleeps badly because of pain, menopause, stress, medication, alcohol, a phone habit they know is not helping, or a life that simply does not leave much room for calm.

In other words, people with insomnia are messy because real life is messy. Some techniques may help a little. Some may irritate you. Some may work for a week, then seem to stop. Some nights will still be poor, even when you have done all the "right" things. And, for some, sleep problems are tied to medical, hormonal, medication-related or stress-related issues that self-help can only partly address.

That does not mean there is nothing you can do. It means this book is not asking you to become perfect at sleep. It is here to help you understand what is happening, try practical changes, and build a better relationship with rest.

The chapters that follow begin with the basics covering how sleep works, why trying too hard can backfire, and how daytime habits affect the night. From there, you will build a small set of tools, including a wind-down routine, breathing techniques, body scan, progressive muscle relaxation, worry dumping, cognitive reframing, and practical ways to handle the 3 AM wake-up. Toward the end, you will bring those pieces together into a personal sleep system that fits your own life.

But it's not a quick fix. If you are looking for a magic pill or a single trick that will give you perfect sleep starting tonight, this is not it. Real improvement takes time, practice and consistency. Many people notice changes within a few weeks, but the process is rarely perfectly straight.

It also means that this isn't a one-size-fits-all plan. You will not use every technique in this book. You will choose the ones that fit your specific challenges and lifestyle. The best way to think about it is as a toolkit, not a rigid protocol.

The goal is not to sleep flawlessly every single night for the rest of your life. That is unrealistic and creates the same performance anxiety that makes sleep worse. The goal is better sleep most of the time, with skills to handle difficult nights when they happen.

If you have a sleep disorder such as sleep apnea or restless legs syndrome, or if you have severe insomnia that does not respond to self-help techniques, you need professional support. Hopefully, this book might also help you recognize when that support is needed.

And remember that if you are on sleep medication then don't stop or reduce it without medical advice.

Quick Start Guide

Sleep Better Tonight

Struggling with sleep right now? You don't need to read the entire book before taking action. This guide gives you immediate steps you can use tonight, plus a simple plan for your first month. Think of this as your roadmap. The full chapters provide the depth and science, but you can start improving your sleep right away.

Tonight: What to Do in the Next Few Hours

1. Try the 4-7-8 Breathing Technique (5-10 minutes before bed)

This is the simplest, most effective technique you can use tonight. When you're ready for bed, sit comfortably and practice this breathing pattern:

- Inhale quietly through your nose for 4 counts

- Hold your breath for 7 counts
- Exhale completely through your mouth for 8 counts
- Repeat this cycle 4-8 times

The extended exhale triggers your body's relaxation response. Don't worry about doing it perfectly. Even a few cycles can help calm your nervous system and prepare you for sleep.

For full instructions and variations, see Chapter 5.

2. Create a Simple 10-Minute Wind-Down (starting 30-60 minutes before bed)

Your body needs a transition period between wakefulness and sleep. Here's the simplest version:

Minutes 1-2: Signal the transition

- Dim all lights in your home
- Put your phone on "Do Not Disturb" mode
- Close your laptop

Minutes 3-5: Gentle movement

- Light stretching
- Slow walking around your home
- Simple tidying (nothing stressful)

Minutes 6-10: Relaxation

- Practice the 4-7-8 breathing above
- Or simply sit quietly and notice your breath

This ritual signals to your body that it's time to shift from activity to rest. Consistency matters more than anything else. Do this at roughly the same time each night.

For the complete wind-down framework, see Chapter 4.

3. Use the 15-Minute Rule If You Wake Up at Night

If you wake during the night and find yourself lying awake:

- Give yourself about 15 minutes to fall back asleep naturally
- If you're still awake and feeling frustrated, get out of bed
- Go to another room if possible (or sit in a chair)
- Do something genuinely boring in very dim light (dull reading, quiet sitting)
- Return to bed only when you feel genuinely sleepy again

This prevents your brain from learning that bed equals wakefulness and frustration. It feels counterintuitive, but it works.

For the complete middle-of-night toolkit, see Chapter 10.

This Week: Your 7-Day Foundation

You don't need to implement everything at once. Here's a realistic week-by-week plan.

Days 1-2: Understand the Science and Mindset

Read: Introduction, Chapters 1-2

Why this matters: You need to understand why trying harder to sleep actually makes it worse. Chapter 1 explains the science of sleep in simple terms. Chapter 2 addresses the performance anxiety that keeps many people awake.

Key insight: Sleep is not a performance. It's something you allow, not something you achieve.

Action: Just read. Let the concepts sink in. Notice if you've been putting pressure on yourself to sleep perfectly.

Days 3-4: Fix Your Daytime Habits

Read: Chapter 3

Implement these three changes:

1. Morning light exposure (10 minutes)

- Get outside within 1 hour of waking
- Even cloudy days work

This sets your internal clock

2. Caffeine cutoff (ideally no caffeine after 2 PM)

- Caffeine has a 5-6 hour half-life
- Afternoon coffee affects nighttime sleep
- Switch to decaf or herbal tea

3. Strategic napping (or avoid entirely)

- If you must nap, limit to 20 minutes before 2 PM
- Long or late naps reduce nighttime sleep pressure
- If you have insomnia, skip naps completely this week

Why this matters: Your daytime habits create the biological foundation for nighttime sleep. You can't compensate for poor daytime choices with perfect bedtime behavior.

Days 5-7: Add One Relaxation Technique

Read: Chapters 5-7 (choose one technique that appeals to you)

Your options:

- 4-7-8 Breathing (Chapter 5): Simplest to start, works quickly, good for anxiety
- Body Scan (Chapter 6): Good for physical tension, helps you notice where you hold stress
- Progressive Muscle Relaxation (Chapter 7): Good for high stress, very physical, creates obvious contrast between tension and relaxation

Don't try all three. Pick one and practice it during your 10-minute wind-down every night this week. You can explore the others later.

Action: Practice your chosen technique for 5-10 minutes as part of your wind-down routine. Remember, falling asleep before you finish is success, not failure.

Throughout the Week: Start the Worry Dump

Read: Chapter 8, Technique 1

Practice: 30-60 minutes before bed, take 5-10 minutes to write down everything on your mind. Don't organize it, don't solve problems, just get it out of your head and onto paper. Then close the notebook.

This externalizes racing thoughts and reduces the cognitive load you bring to bed. Research shows this simple practice can reduce sleep onset time by an average of 9 minutes.

Why it works: Your mind races at bedtime because it finally has space to process the day. The worry dump gives it that space earlier, so bedtime can be for sleep, not problem-solving.

Week 2: Optimize Your Environment

Read: Chapter 9

Complete the 10-minute sleep environment audit

Check these five factors:

1. Temperature: 60-68°F (ideally 65-68°F)
2. Light: Complete darkness (blackout curtains or eye mask)
3. Sound: Below 35 decibels (earplugs or white noise if needed)
4. Comfort: Supportive mattress and appropriate pillows
5. Association: Bed used only for sleep and intimacy

Action: Make 1-3 budget-friendly improvements based on your audit. Most changes cost less than $50 and some are free.

Why this matters: Environmental factors affect sleep through both physiological pathways (temperature, light) and psychological associations (stimulus control). These changes often produce immediate results.

Week 3: Build Your Personal System

Read: Chapter 11

Complete these steps:

1. Identify your primary sleep challenge

- Sleep onset difficulty (can't fall asleep initially)
- Sleep maintenance difficulty (wake during night)
- Mixed insomnia (both onset and maintenance)
- Sleep anxiety (fear of not sleeping)

2. Choose 3-4 core techniques based on your challenge

Chapter 11 provides specific recommendations for each type

3. Create your consistent schedule

- Same bedtime and wake time (even weekends)
- Same wind-down routine
- Same relaxation technique

Action: Write down your personal sleep system. What time will you start your wind-down? Which techniques will you use? What's your plan for middle-of-night awakenings?

Why this matters: Random technique application is less effective than a consistent, personalized system. You're building habits, not just trying tricks.

Week 4 and Beyond: Maintain and Troubleshoot

Read: Chapter 12
Focus on:

- Consistency over perfection (the 80/20 rule)
- Handling setbacks without catastrophizing
- Adapting your system to life changes
- Knowing when to seek professional help

Action: Continue your system. Track your progress simply (how you feel, not detailed metrics). Adjust techniques if needed, but give changes at least a week before switching.

Why this matters: Sleep improvement takes time. Most people see noticeable changes within 2-4 weeks of consistent practice. Some techniques work immediately, others take longer. Both are normal.

If You Have Specific Challenges

Jump to these chapters as needed:

- Middle-of-night awakenings: Chapter 10
- Racing thoughts at bedtime: Chapter 8
- Bed partner issues: Chapter 9
- Sleep anxiety or perfectionism: Chapter 2
- Considering sleep restriction therapy: Chapter 11 (advanced technique, use with caution)

The Most Important Thing to Remember

You don't need to do everything perfectly. In fact, trying to be perfect about sleep makes it worse. That's the central message of this entire book.

Start with the basics above. Be patient with yourself. Build gradually. Some nights will be better than others, and that's completely normal.

Good enough sleep is good enough.

Sleep improvement is not linear. You might have a great night followed by a rough night. This doesn't mean you're failing or that the techniques don't work. It means you're human and sleep is influenced by many factors, not all of which you control.

What you can control:

- Your daytime habits
- Your wind-down routine
- Your response to poor sleep
- Your mindset about sleep

What you can't control:

- Exactly when you fall asleep
- Waking during the night
- Your sleep stages
- How you feel every single morning

Focus on what you can control. Let go of what you can't.

Three Paths Through This Book

Choose the method that fits your needs:

Path 1: The Linear Reader Read from Introduction through Chapter 12 in order. This gives you the complete understanding of sleep science, techniques, and system-building.

Path 2: The Action-Oriented Reader Use this Quick Start Guide tonight. Read technique chapters (4-8) first and start practicing. Read the science chapters (1-3) when you're ready for deeper understanding.

Path 3: The Anxious Reader Read Chapter 2 first. It will change how you think about sleep and reduce the pressure you're putting on yourself. Then follow the Quick Start Guide and read other chapters as needed.

All three paths work. Choose what feels right for you.

Ready to Begin?

Tonight, try the 4-7-8 breathing and a simple wind-down routine. That's it. Don't overthink it, don't try to do everything at once, and don't judge yourself if it doesn't work perfectly the first time.

Your sleep can improve. And you don't have to try so hard.

Now, let's look at the details. Turn to Chapter 1 to understand why these techniques work, or jump straight to Chapter 4 if you want to build your wind-down routine first.

The choice is yours. There's no wrong way to use this book.

Part 1: Understanding Sleep (Without the Anxiety)

Chapter 1

The Science of Sleep

Sarah, 28, lies in bed scrolling through her sleep tracking app for the third time tonight. According to the data, she only got 6 hours and 42 minutes of sleep last night, with only 47 minutes of deep sleep. Her heart rate was elevated. Her sleep score: a disappointing 62 out of 100. Now, at 11:37 PM, she's wide awake, anxious about getting enough sleep tonight, and whether tomorrow will be another exhausted, foggy day.

Meanwhile, across town, David, 58, wakes up for the fourth time tonight. He checks the clock: 3:15 AM. He's been waking up earlier and earlier each morning, and falling asleep during afternoon meetings has become embarrassing. His doctor says his sleep is "normal for his age," but David remembers sleeping soundly through the night in his thirties. What changed?

Both Sarah and David are experiencing sleep problems, but for different reasons. Understanding why sleep becomes difficult, whether you're dealing with modern anxiety or age-related changes, is the first step toward actually fixing it and you don't need a PhD in neuroscience to understand what's happening. You just need about ten minutes.

What Actually Happens When You Sleep

Sleep is not an on-off switch. Your brain doesn't simply power down for eight hours and reboot in the morning. Instead, sleep is an active, dynamic process where your brain cycles through distinct stages, each serving different purposes.

Throughout the night, you move through roughly 90-minute cycles, each containing four stages. The first three stages are collectively called non-REM (NREM) sleep, and they progress from light to deep sleep. The fourth stage is REM (rapid eye movement) sleep, where most vivid dreaming occurs.

Here's what happens in each stage

Stage 1 (Light Sleep): This is the transition between wakefulness and sleep, lasting only a few minutes. Your heartbeat, breathing, and eye movements slow down, and your muscles relax. You can be easily awakened during this stage.

Stage 2 (Deeper Light Sleep): Your body temperature drops, eye movements stop, and brain waves slow down with occasional bursts of rapid activity called sleep spindles. This stage makes up about 50% of your total sleep time. Research suggests that sleep spindles play a role in memory consolidation and protecting sleep from external disturbances.

Stage 3 (Deep Sleep or Slow-Wave Sleep): This is the most restorative stage. Your brain produces slow delta waves, and it becomes much harder to wake you up. Deep sleep is when your body does its most important repair work, building bone and muscle, strengthening the immune system, and clearing metabolic waste from the brain. This stage is crucial for feeling refreshed in the morning.

REM Sleep: Your brain becomes more active, almost as active as when you're awake. Your eyes move rapidly behind closed eyelids (hence the name), your breathing becomes faster and irregular, and your heart rate increases. Most of your muscles become temporarily paralyzed to prevent you from acting out your dreams. REM sleep is essential for emotional regulation, memory consolidation, and creativity.

As the night progresses, the balance shifts. Early in the night, you spend more time in deep sleep. As morning approaches, you spend more time in REM sleep and lighter stages. This is why being woken up early in the morning often interrupts a dream, while waking in the middle of the night might leave you feeling groggy - you were likely in deep sleep.

THE TWO FORCES THAT CONTROL YOUR SLEEP

Understanding what makes up sleep is helpful, but it doesn't explain why you feel sleepy at certain times and alert at others. Two powerful biological systems work together to regulate when you sleep and wake. Think of them as two separate clocks that need to stay synchronized.

Sleep Pressure: Your Biological Battery

The first system is called sleep-wake homeostasis, or more simply, sleep pressure. From the moment you wake up, a chemical called adenosine begins accumulating in your brain. The longer you're awake, the more adenosine builds up, and the sleepier you feel. It's like a battery slowly draining throughout the day.

When you sleep, your brain clears away this adenosine, "recharging" the battery. This is why you feel refreshed after a good night's sleep - you've cleared the sleep debt. It's also why pulling an all-nighter makes you feel progressively worse: the adenosine just keeps building with no opportunity to clear it.

Here's an interesting detail: caffeine works by blocking adenosine receptors in your brain. It doesn't actually give you energy, it just prevents you from feeling the sleepiness that's already there. The adenosine is still accumulating; you just can't sense it. When the caffeine wears off, all that built-up adenosine hits you at once, causing the dreaded "caffeine crash."

Your Circadian Rhythm: Your Internal Clock

The second system is your circadian rhythm, a roughly 24-hour internal clock located in a tiny region of your brain called the suprachiasmatic nucleus (SCN). This cluster of about 20,000 cells in your hypothalamus acts as your body's master timekeeper, coordinating when you feel alert and when you feel sleepy.

Your circadian rhythm doesn't just control sleep. It influences body temperature, hormone release, hunger, digestion, and even how well your immune system functions. It's why you tend to feel hungry around the same times each day, and why jet lag feels so disorienting because your internal clock is out of sync with the external world.

The most powerful cue for your circadian rhythm is light, especially the blue wavelengths present in morning sunlight. When light enters your eyes, it sends signals to the SCN in your brain, essentially saying, "It's daytime, time to be awake." This suppresses the production of melatonin, a hormone that promotes sleepiness. As evening arrives and light fades, melatonin production increases, signaling that it's time to wind down.

This is why staring at bright screens late at night can interfere with sleep. The blue light from phones, tablets, and computers tricks your brain into thinking it's still daytime, suppressing melatonin and delaying sleepiness. Your circadian rhythm gets confused, making it harder to fall asleep at your intended bedtime.

When the Two Systems Work Together (and When They Don't)

Ideally, sleep pressure and your circadian rhythm work in harmony. As adenosine builds throughout the day, your circadian rhythm simultaneously prepares your body for sleep as evening approaches. By bedtime, both systems are tuned to each other, making it easy to fall asleep.

But modern life often disrupts this synchronization. Irregular sleep schedules, insufficient daylight exposure, late-night screen time, and stress can throw these systems out of balance. When sleep pressure says "sleep now" but your circadian rhythm says "stay awake," you end up lying in bed, exhausted but unable to sleep. Or you might fall asleep easily but wake up in the middle of the night when your circadian rhythm mistakenly signals that it's time to be alert.

Understanding these two systems is crucial because many of the techniques in this book work by either building appropriate sleep pressure or realigning your circadian rhythm, or both.

Why Sleep Is Harder in the Modern World (For Everyone)

If sleep is such a fundamental biological need, why do so many people struggle with it? The answer is that our modern environment is fundamentally mismatched with our biology. Our brains evolved for a world very different from the one we live in today.

The Light Problem

For most of human history, our ancestors' exposure to light was dictated by the sun. Daylight signaled activity; darkness signaled rest. The invention of artificial lighting changed everything. We now have access to bright light at any hour, which confuses our circadian rhythms. Research shows that many adults, especially those who work indoors, get less than an hour of natural daylight exposure per day. Without sufficient bright light during the day, the circadian signal becomes weak and unreliable.

At night, the problem reverses. Our ancestors experienced true darkness, which allowed melatonin to rise naturally. Today, we're surrounded by light, from the streetlights outside, lamps inside, to the bright glow of screens. Even dim light at night can suppress melatonin production by up to 50%, making it harder to fall asleep.

The Stress and Connectivity Problem

Our stress response system, often called the "fight-or-flight" response, evolved to handle immediate physical threats: a predator, a rival, a dangerous situation. When activated, this system floods your body with cortisol and adrenaline, increasing heart rate, sharpening focus, and preparing you to take action. Once the threat passed, the system would calm down.

Today, threats are rarely physical and rarely resolve quickly. Work deadlines, financial worries, relationship conflicts, and global news create chronic, low-level stress that keeps the fight-or-flight system partially activated. Your body remains in a state of vigilance, making it difficult to relax enough to sleep.

The problem is compounded by constant connectivity. Smartphones mean we're always reachable, always aware of what's happening, always able to check just one more email or scroll through one more social media feed. This creates a sense of urgency and stimulation that directly opposes the calm, quiet state needed for sleep. Research indicates that nearly 40% of adults aged 18-29 report experiencing sleep-related anxiety at least three times per week, often linked to digital device use and social media consumption.

The Problem of Trying Too Hard

Here's where things get particularly tricky for people like Sarah, our anxious sleep tracker. Sleep is unique among biological functions because it requires a certain passivity. You can't force yourself to sleep the way you can force yourself to eat or exercise. The harder you try, the more elusive sleep becomes.

This creates a vicious cycle. A few bad nights lead to anxiety about sleep. That anxiety activates your stress response, making sleep even more difficult. You start monitoring your sleep obsessively, checking apps and devices, calculating hours, worrying about getting enough deep sleep or REM sleep. Each night becomes a performance you're afraid of failing.

This phenomenon has become so common that researchers have given it a name: orthosomnia, derived from the Greek words for "correct" and "sleep." It's the unhealthy obsession with achieving perfect sleep, often driven by sleep tracking technology. Studies published in the Journal of Clinical Sleep Medicine have documented cases where people's anxiety about their sleep data actually caused insomnia, even when their objective sleep quality was normal.

The irony is profound: the tools designed to improve sleep can make it worse by creating performance anxiety. This is why this book takes an explicitly anti-perfectionism approach. Good sleep doesn't come from optimization but from relaxation.

Why Sleep Gets Harder as You Age

If you're over 40, you may have noticed that sleep isn't as easy as it used to be. You're not imagining it. Aging brings real, measurable changes to sleep, and understanding these changes can help you adapt rather than fight against your biology.

Your Internal Clock Shifts Forward

As people age, the SCN, that part of your brain that contains 'the master clock', begins to deteriorate slightly. This doesn't mean it stops working, but it does become less robust. One of the most noticeable effects is a phenomenon called phase advance: your circadian rhythm shifts earlier.

In practical terms, this means you start feeling tired earlier in the evening and waking up earlier in the morning. Research shows that this shift typically begins around age 60-65, though some people notice it earlier. If you used to be a night owl who could easily stay up until midnight, you might find yourself yawning at 9 PM. If you once slept until 7 or 8 AM, you might now wake at 5 or 6 AM, unable to fall back asleep.

This isn't insomnia but your circadian rhythm recalibrating. The problem is that social expectations haven't shifted. If you're still working or have evening commitments, going to bed at 9 PM isn't always practical. This creates a mismatch between your biology and your schedule, leading to insufficient sleep.

Your Sleep Architecture Changes

Sleep itself becomes lighter and more fragmented with age. Studies tracking brain activity during sleep have found that older adults spend significantly less time in deep, slow-wave sleep (Stage 3) and more time in lighter stages. By age 60, the percentage of deep sleep decreases by about 2% per decade compared to younger adults.

This means you're more easily awakened by noise, light, discomfort, or the need to use the bathroom. You might wake up multiple times during the night, even if you don't fully remember these awakenings in the morning. While you may spend the same amount of time in bed, the quality and continuity of your sleep decline.

REM sleep also changes, though less dramatically. Older adults tend to have shorter REM periods and may experience them earlier in the night rather than concentrated toward morning.

Your Body Produces Less Melatonin

Melatonin, the hormone that signals sleepiness, decreases with age. Older adults produce less melatonin overall, and the nighttime surge in melatonin becomes less pronounced. This makes it harder for the body to generate a strong "time to sleep" signal.

Additionally, older adults often get less exposure to bright daylight, averaging only about one hour per day according to research. This is especially true for those with limited mobility, those living in care facilities, or those with conditions like Alzheimer's disease. Without sufficient bright light during the day, the circadian signal becomes even weaker, creating a vicious cycle of poor sleep.

Health Conditions and Medications Complicate Things

Sleep problems in older adults are often compounded by health conditions that become more common with age. Arthritis, heart disease, diabetes, chronic pain, anxiety, and depression can all interfere with sleep. The relationship is bidirectional: poor sleep worsens these conditions, and these conditions worsen sleep.

Medications add another layer of complexity. Nearly 40% of adults over 65 take five or more medications, and many of these can affect sleep, either by causing drowsiness at the wrong times, interfering with sleep architecture, or creating side effects like nighttime urination. The interactions between multiple medications can also produce unexpected effects on sleep.

The Good News: Sleep Problems Aren't Inevitable

Here's what's important to understand: while aging does change sleep, it doesn't mean you're doomed to poor sleep. The notion that "older people need less sleep" is a myth. Adults of all ages need roughly seven to nine hours of sleep per night. The difference is that older adults often have a harder time getting that sleep, not that they need less of it.

Many sleep problems attributed to aging are actually caused by things we can change. For example, insufficient light exposure, lack of physical activity, poor sleep habits, untreated health conditions, or medication side effects.

The techniques in this book are designed to work with your biology, not against it.

The Relaxation Response: Your Secret Weapon

Now that you understand what makes sleep difficult, let's talk about what makes it easier. This is something called the relaxation response and it's the physiological opposite of the stress response.

When you're stressed or anxious, your sympathetic nervous system activates. This is the "fight-or-flight" system: heart rate increases, breathing becomes shallow and rapid, muscles tense, and stress hormones flood your body. This state is incompatible with sleep.

The relaxation response activates your parasympathetic nervous system, sometimes called the "rest-and-digest" system. Heart rate slows, breathing deepens, muscles relax, and your body shifts into a state of calm. This is the state that allows sleep to happen.

Here's the crucial insight: you can deliberately activate the relaxation response. It's not something that just happens to you, it's something you can practice and strengthen. Every technique in this book, breathing exercises, body scans, progressive muscle relaxation, cognitive reframing, works by activating this response.

The relaxation response was first described by Dr. Herbert Benson at Harvard Medical School in the 1970s. His research showed that simple techniques like focused breathing and meditation could produce measurable physiological changes: lower blood pressure, reduced heart rate, decreased muscle tension, and changes in brain wave patterns consistent with relaxation. Subsequent research has confirmed that these techniques are highly effective for improving sleep, particularly when combined with cognitive-behavioral strategies.

The beauty of this is that it's a skill you can learn and the more you practice it, the easier it becomes. Over time, your body learns to shift into this state more quickly and more completely, and it's why the 10-minute techniques in this book become more effective the more you use them.

The Sleep Anxiety Trap (and How to Escape It)

Let's return to Sarah and her sleep tracking app. What's happening to her is a perfect example of how anxiety about sleep creates a self-fulfilling prophecy.

Here's the cycle:

1. A few bad nights (perhaps due to stress, travel, or just random variation - everyone has occasional poor sleep)

2. Worry about sleep ("What if I can't sleep tonight? What if I'm tired tomorrow?")
3. Hypervigilance (monitoring every sensation, checking the clock, tracking data obsessively)
4. Increased arousal (worry activates the stress response, making sleep physiologically more difficult)
5. Poor sleep (confirming the fear and strengthening the anxiety)
6. More worry (the cycle repeats and intensifies)

This is called psychophysiological insomnia, and it's one of the most common forms of chronic sleep problems. The original trigger - whatever caused those first few bad nights - may be long gone, but the anxiety perpetuates the problem.

The way out of this trap is counterintuitive: you have to stop trying so hard. You have to let go of the need for perfect sleep. You have to accept that some nights will be better than others, and that's okay. This doesn't mean giving up or resigning yourself to poor sleep. It means shifting from a mindset of control and performance to one of allowing and acceptance.

Research on Cognitive Behavioral Therapy for Insomnia (CBT-I) consistently shows that addressing anxious thoughts about sleep is one of the most effective interventions. Studies have found that CBT-I is more effective than sleeping pills for long-term improvement, with benefits lasting years after treatment ends. In fact, clinical studies show that CBT-I can improve long-term sleep for around 70–80 per cent of people who follow its methods. It works so well both in the short and longer term that it is recommended as the first line of defense against insomnia from the American College of Physicians, the European Sleep Research Society, the Australasian Sleep Association, to the Department of Veterans' Affairs/Department of Defense (VA/DOD).

This is why Chapter 2 of this book focuses entirely on the anti-perfectionism mindset. Before you learn any techniques, you need to change your relationship with sleep. You need to understand that "good enough" sleep is actually good enough, and that the pursuit of perfect sleep is often what stands in your way.

What About Sleep Medications?

Before we move forward, let's address a question many readers have: "Should I be taking medication for my sleep problems?"

This is a legitimate question, and the answer is nuanced. Sleep medications can be helpful in certain situations, but they have limitations.

When Medications Might Be Appropriate

Sleep medications can provide short-term relief during acute crises and are often very helpful but, they aren't great for long-term use.

Any of the following, might be recommended for short-term use:

1. Temporary high-stress situations: A death in the family, job loss, divorce, or other major life events that temporarily disrupt sleep.
2. Short-term insomnia: A few nights or weeks of poor sleep that hasn't become chronic.
3. Severe insomnia with significant impairment: When sleep problems are so severe that they're affecting your safety or ability to function, and you need immediate relief while working on longer-term solutions.

In these situations, a doctor might prescribe sleep medication for a limited time (typically 2-4 weeks). This can break the cycle of anxiety and sleep deprivation while you implement behavioral changes.

However, sleep medications have significant drawbacks for long-term use:

- They don't address the underlying causes. Medications can help you fall asleep, but they don't fix the behavioral, cognitive, or environmental factors that are causing your insomnia. When you stop taking them, the insomnia often returns.
- Tolerance also develops. Over time, your body adapts to the medication and you need higher doses to get the same effect. This is true for both prescription sleep aids and over-the-counter options like diphenhydramine (Benadryl).
- As you might have guessed, dependence can occur too. Your body can become dependent on the medication to sleep, making it difficult to stop and withdrawal can temporarily worsen insomnia, which reinforces the belief that you need the medication.
- Sleep quality is also altered because most sleep medications change your sleep architecture. They may help you fall asleep faster or stay asleep longer, but the sleep you get is not the same as natural sleep and some medications suppress REM sleep or deep sleep.
- Side effects are common with daytime grogginess, impaired thinking, increased fall risk (especially in older adults), and next-day performance impairment.

And then we might experience rebound insomnia. When you stop taking sleep medications, especially if you stop suddenly, insomnia often gets temporarily worse. This can last for several days to weeks.

The Research on Behavioral Techniques vs. Medications

Multiple studies have compared Cognitive Behavioral Therapy for Insomnia (CBT-I, the foundation of this book) to sleep medications.

The findings are consistent:

1. Short-term: Medications work faster. You might see improvement in a few days rather than 2-4 weeks.
2. Long-term: CBT-I is more effective. Benefits persist long after treatment ends, while medication benefits disappear when you stop taking them.
3. Side effects: CBT-I does not carry the medication-related side effects associated with sleep drugs

Combination: Using both together can be helpful in the short term, but the goal should be to ease off medication while maintaining the behavioral changes.

Because of this evidence, major medical organizations now recommend CBT-I as the first-line treatment for chronic insomnia, before medications.

If you're considering sleep medication, it is worth speaking with your doctor about CBT-I and behavioral approaches, which are often recommended as a first-line treatment for chronic insomnia.

In fact, learning behavioral techniques may give you more options to discuss with your doctor, especially if you want to reduce reliance on medication over time.

Whatever you do, don't stop suddenly. Quitting sleep medications cold turkey can cause rebound insomnia and other withdrawal effects. Work with your doctor to taper gradually.

- Implement techniques while still on medication. Start using the strategies in this book while you're still taking your medication. Once the behavioral changes are working, you can slowly reduce the medication dose under medical supervision.

- Expect temporary worsening. As you reduce your medication, you might have a few rough nights. This is normal and temporary. The behavioral techniques will become more effective as your body adjusts to sleeping without medication.

Sleep medications can be a useful short-term tool in specific situations, but they're not a long-term solution. The techniques in this book can help address many of the habits, thoughts and patterns that keep insomnia going, and they do not carry the medication-related side effects associated with sleep drugs,

A Few Things to Hold Onto

You don't need to memorize everything in this chapter. Here are the key takeaways:

Sleep is an active process with distinct stages, each serving important functions. You cycle through these stages multiple times per night.

Two systems control your sleep: sleep pressure (which builds the longer you're awake) and your circadian rhythm (your internal 24-hour clock). When these systems are aligned and functioning well, sleep comes naturally.

Modern life disrupts these systems through insufficient daylight, excessive artificial light at night, chronic stress, and constant connectivity. These aren't personal failings, but rather environmental challenges that affect almost everyone.

Aging changes sleep by changing your circadian rhythm, making sleep lighter and disrupted, and reducing melatonin production. These changes are real, but they don't mean you need less sleep or that poor sleep is inevitable.

Trying too hard makes sleep worse. Sleep requires relaxation, not effort. Anxiety about sleep activates your stress response, which is physiologically incompatible with sleep.

The relaxation response is your tool. You can actively trigger your parasympathetic nervous system through simple techniques, making sleep easier and more natural.

Good sleep comes from working with your biology, not fighting it. The techniques in this book are designed to realign your sleep systems, reduce anxiety, and create the conditions that allow sleep to happen naturally.

Now that you understand the science, you're ready to change your mindset. In the next chapter, we'll tackle the single biggest obstacle to better sleep: the belief that you need to be perfect at it.

Chapter 2

Stop Trying So Hard (The Anti-Perfectionism Mindset)

Marcus sits in his doctor's office, exhausted. "I'm doing everything right," he says, scrolling through his sleep app. "I go to bed at the same time every night. I avoid caffeine after noon. I keep my bedroom cool and dark. I even bought blackout curtains and a white noise machine. But I still can't sleep. What am I doing wrong?"

His doctor looks at the app on Marcus's phone, which shows detailed graphs of his sleep stages, heart rate variability, and a sleep score of 68 out of 100, highlighted in red. "How do you feel when you see that red number?" she asks.

"Anxious," Marcus admits. "Like I'm failing at something that should be natural."

"That," his doctor says gently, "is exactly the problem."

Marcus has fallen into one of the most common traps in modern sleep culture - the belief that sleep is something you can perfect through effort and optimization. He's not alone. As we discussed in Chapter 1, the phenomenon of orthosomnia - the obsessive pursuit of perfect sleep - has become increasingly common, particularly among people who use sleep tracking devices. The irony is that the harder Marcus tries to achieve perfect sleep, the more elusive it becomes.

This chapter is about learning to do the opposite. It's about letting go of perfectionism, releasing the need for control, and understanding that "good enough" sleep is not only sufficient, it's often better than the exhausting pursuit of perfection.

The Performance Paradox

Sleep is fundamentally different from almost every other goal you might pursue. If you want to run faster, you train harder. If you want to learn a skill, you practice more. If you want to excel at work, you put in more effort. In nearly every domain of life, trying harder produces better results.

Sleep is the exception. Sleep requires surrender, not effort. As we know from Chapter 1, sleep happens when your parasympathetic nervous system takes over (this is the "rest and digest" system which we will also call the 'relaxation response'). But trying to force sleep activates the opposite system and it triggers the sympathetic nervous system, your "fight or flight" response. It means that the very act of trying creates the physiological state that prevents sleep.

This creates what researchers call the performance paradox of insomnia. The more you care about sleeping well, the more pressure you put on yourself to succeed, and the harder it becomes to actually sleep. Studies examining cognitive arousal in insomnia patients have found that the effort to control sleep is itself a primary factor in chronic insomnia.

Think about other automatic bodily functions. You don't try to digest your food, it happens naturally. You don't consciously regulate your heart rate during rest, your body does it for you. You can't force yourself to feel hungry or thirsty on command. Sleep is the same. It's a biological process that occurs naturally when the conditions are right and when you're not interfering with it.

The moment you start treating sleep as a performance to be evaluated, you've introduced the very anxiety that disrupts it.

The Myth of Perfect Sleep

Let's address a fundamental misconception - there is no such thing as perfect sleep.

Even people who consider themselves "good sleepers" don't sleep perfectly every night. Research using objective sleep monitoring has shown that everyone experiences night-to-night variability in sleep duration, sleep quality, and time spent in different sleep stages. A study tracking healthy adults with no sleep complaints found that their sleep varied by up to 90 minutes from night to night, and their percentage of deep sleep fluctuated significantly.

This variation is normal because your sleep is influenced by dozens of factors from what you ate, how much you moved, what stressors you encountered, where you are in your menstrual cycle (if applicable), the temperature and noise in your environment, and even random biological variation. Some nights you'll sleep deeply while other nights will be lighter and more broken. This is how human sleep works.

The problem arises when you interpret normal variation as failure. When your sleep tracking app gives you a score of 68, it's not telling you that you failed, it's telling you that you had a night that fell within the normal range of human sleep variation. But the red color and the number below 70 trigger anxiety, which then makes the next night's sleep more difficult, creating a self-fulfilling prophecy.

Here's what perfect sleep actually looks like - it's variable, sometimes deep and sometimes light, occasionally interrupted, and generally sufficient to allow you to function reasonably well during the day. That's it. That's the goal.

Common Dysfunctional Beliefs About Sleep

Research on Cognitive Behavioral Therapy for Insomnia (CBT-I) has identified several common beliefs about sleep that, while they seem reasonable on the surface, actually maintain and worsen sleep problems. These are called dysfunctional beliefs about sleep, and recognizing them is the first step toward changing them.

Belief 1: "I need exactly 8 hours of sleep every night."

Why it's problematic: While seven to nine hours is the recommended range for most adults, individual sleep needs vary. Some people function well on seven hours; others need closer to nine. Moreover, your sleep need varies from night to night based on physical activity, stress, and other factors. Rigidly insisting on exactly eight hours creates pressure and anxiety.

More helpful belief: "Most adults need somewhere between seven and nine hours. I'll aim for that range and pay attention to how I feel, rather than fixating on a specific number."

Belief 2: "If I don't get enough sleep tonight, tomorrow will be ruined."

Why it's problematic: This catastrophic thinking creates enormous pressure. While poor sleep certainly isn't pleasant, research shows that people consistently overestimate how much it will impair their next-day functioning. Studies have found that the correlation between objective sleep quality and next-day performance is often weaker than people expect. Much of the impairment comes from anxiety about having slept poorly, not from the poor sleep itself.

More helpful belief: "A bad night's sleep is unpleasant, but I've functioned after poor sleep before and I can do it again. One night won't ruin me."

Belief 3: "I have no control over my sleep."

Why it's problematic: This belief creates helplessness and hopelessness, which increase anxiety and depression, both of which worsen sleep. While you can't directly control sleep (remember, it's not a performance), you can absolutely influence the conditions that make sleep more likely.

More helpful belief: "I can't force myself to sleep, but I can create conditions that make sleep more likely. I have influence, even if I don't have direct control."

Belief 4: "I must get a certain amount of deep sleep or REM sleep."

Why it's problematic: This belief is a direct product of sleep tracking technology. While deep sleep and REM sleep serve important functions, your body naturally regulates how much of each stage you get based on your needs. Worrying about specific sleep stages adds another layer of performance anxiety and ignores the fact that consumer sleep trackers are often inaccurate in detecting sleep stages.

More helpful belief: "My body knows how to regulate sleep stages. If I create good conditions for sleep overall, my brain will cycle through the stages it needs."

Belief 5: "If I'm awake in the middle of the night, I should try harder to fall back asleep."

Why it's problematic: From Chapter 1 we know that middle-of-the-night awakenings are normal, especially as you age. Trying harder to fall back asleep activates your stress response and makes sleep less likely. This is where the performance paradox is most obvious.

More helpful belief: "Waking up during the night is normal. If I'm awake for more than about 10 minutes, I'll get up and do something boring until I feel sleepy again. Rest is still valuable even if I'm not asleep."

Belief 6: "My sleep problems are unique and unfixable."

Why it's problematic: This belief creates a sense of isolation and hopelessness. In reality, sleep problems are extremely common with between 40% and 70% of older adults experiencing chronic sleep issues, and sleep-related anxiety affects nearly 40% of younger adults. You are not alone.

More helpful belief: "Sleep problems are common and treatable. Many people have improved their sleep using the same techniques I'm learning."

Exercise 1: Identifying Your Sleep Beliefs (5-10 minutes)

Let's make this practical. Take a few minutes right now to identify your own beliefs about sleep. You'll need paper and a pen, or you can use your phone's notes app.

Step 1: Think about the last time you had a bad night's sleep. What thoughts went through your mind as you lay awake? What did you think about the next morning? Write down at least three specific thoughts.

Examples:

"I'll never fall asleep now."
"I'm going to be exhausted tomorrow."
"Why can everyone else sleep except me?"
"I'm ruining my health by not sleeping."

Step 2: For each thought, ask yourself these questions:

Is this thought completely true, or is it an exaggeration?
What evidence do I have for and against this thought?
What would I tell a friend who had this thought?
Is this thought helpful, or does it make me more anxious?

Step 3: Rewrite each thought in a more balanced, helpful way.

Here are a couple of examples:

Original thought: "I'll never fall asleep now."

Evidence check: "I've had many nights where I thought I wouldn't sleep but eventually did. Even when I don't sleep well, I survive the next day."

Reframed thought: "I'm having trouble falling asleep right now, but that doesn't mean I won't sleep at all. Even if tonight is difficult, I'll get through tomorrow."

This exercise is adapted from cognitive restructuring techniques used in CBT-I. Research has shown that changing dysfunctional beliefs about sleep is one of the most effective components of insomnia treatment with multiple studies finding that cognitive therapy targeting sleep beliefs produced moderate to large improvements in insomnia symptoms.

The "Good Enough" Sleep Log

Here's a radical idea. What if you stopped tracking your sleep metrics and started tracking how you actually feel?

Most sleep tracking focuses on objective data: hours slept, sleep stages, heart rate, movement. But this data often creates more anxiety than insight. Consumer sleep trackers are notoriously inaccurate at detecting sleep stages, with error rates of 20-30% compared to clinical measuring (called polysomnography, or PSG). You might be getting perfectly adequate sleep, but your device tells you otherwise, triggering anxiety that then disrupts your sleep.

Instead, try tracking what actually matters: your subjective experience and daytime functioning.

How to Keep a "Good Enough" Sleep Log

Each morning, answer just three simple questions. Don't overthink them, your first instinct is usually the most accurate.

1. How do I feel this morning? Rate on a simple scale:

- Refreshed
- Okay
- Tired but functional
- Exhausted

2. How well did I function yesterday? Consider your energy, mood, concentration, and ability to do what you needed to do.

- Functioned well
- Functioned adequately
- Struggled but got through it
- Could barely function

3. Did I worry about sleep yesterday or last night?

- Not at all
- A little
- Quite a bit
- Constantly

That's it. No sleep scores. No graphs. No red numbers. Just three simple questions about your actual experience.

After a week or two, you'll likely notice that the relationship between how you think you slept and how you actually function is often weaker than you expected. You might have nights where you felt like you barely slept, but you functioned fine the next day. Or nights where your sleep felt okay, but you struggled with energy. This helps break the catastrophic thinking that one bad night will ruin you.

You'll also notice patterns. Perhaps you worry most about sleep on Sunday nights before the work week. Or maybe your anxiety about sleep is worse than the actual sleep problem. These insights are far more valuable than knowing you got 47 minutes of deep sleep versus 52 minutes.

Exercise 2: The Permission Slip (5 minutes)

This exercise might feel silly, but it's surprisingly powerful. You're going to write yourself a permission slip - yes, like the ones from school - giving yourself permission to have imperfect sleep.

Here's a template, but feel free to modify it to fit your situation:

PERMISSION SLIP

I, ______________ [your name], hereby give myself permission to:

- Have nights where I don't sleep well
- Wake up during the night without panicking
- Sleep less than 8 hours sometimes
- Not track my sleep obsessively
- Feel tired occasionally without catastrophizing
- Be human, with all the normal variation that entails

I acknowledge that:

- Sleep is not a performance
- "Good enough" sleep is actually good enough
- My worth is not determined by my sleep score
- Trying too hard makes sleep worse, not better

I commit to:

- Being kind to myself on difficult nights
- Focusing on creating good conditions for sleep rather than forcing sleep to happen
- Measuring success by how I feel and function, not by numbers on an app.

Signed: ______________________

Date: ______________________

Keep this permission slip somewhere you'll see it, perhaps on your nightstand or as a photo on your phone. When you find yourself spiraling into sleep anxiety, read it. Remind yourself that you've given yourself permission to be imperfect.

This might seem like a trivial exercise, but it's based on acceptance-based approaches to insomnia. Research on Acceptance and Commitment Therapy for Insomnia (ACT-I) has shown that increasing willingness to experience sleep-related discomfort, rather than fighting against it, significantly improves sleep outcomes. A study published in 2023 found that ACT-based interventions had significant effects on primary insomnia and anxiety symptoms, particularly among people with high sleep-related anxiety.

The Paradoxical Intention Technique

Now let's talk about one of the most counterintuitive, and effective, techniques for sleep anxiety - trying to stay awake.

Paradoxical intention is a technique developed in the 1970s specifically for people who experience anxiety about falling asleep. The instruction is simple: when you get into bed, instead of trying to fall asleep, gently try to stay awake. Keep your eyes open. Notice the room around you. Don't do anything stimulating, no reading, no screens, no getting up, just lie there and try to remain awake.

Why does this work? Because it removes the performance pressure. You're no longer trying to achieve sleep, which means you're no longer anxious about failing to achieve it. Without that anxiety, your parasympathetic nervous system can activate, and sleep becomes possible.

Research on paradoxical intention has shown it to be effective for reducing sleep onset latency (the time it takes to fall asleep) and decreasing anxiety about sleep. A systematic review and meta-analysis published in 2022 found that paradoxical intention produced significant improvements in insomnia symptoms, particularly for people with sleep onset difficulties.

The key is the word "gently." You're not forcing yourself to stay awake with effort, that would just activate your stress response in a different direction. You're simply letting go of the goal of falling asleep. You're giving yourself permission to be awake without judgment or anxiety.

How to Practice Paradoxical Intention

1. Get into bed at your normal bedtime, having completed your wind-down routine (we'll cover this in Chapter 3).
2. Lie in a comfortable position with your eyes open.
3. Say to yourself, silently: "I'm going to stay awake and notice what it feels like to rest in bed. There's no pressure to fall asleep."
4. Keep your eyes open and gently observe your surroundings. Notice the shadows on the ceiling, the quality of the darkness, the sounds in the room.
5. If your eyes start to feel heavy, don't fight it, but don't actively try to close them either. Just notice the sensation.
6. If you find yourself thinking "Am I falling asleep yet?" or "Is this working?", gently redirect your attention back to simply staying awake and resting.

Most people find that within 10-20 minutes, their eyes close naturally and they drift off. The technique works precisely because you've stopped trying.

Reframing "Bad Nights"

You will still have difficult nights. This is normal. The question is: how do you think about those nights?

The way you interpret a bad night determines whether it becomes an isolated incident or the beginning of a spiral. Catastrophic thinking ("I'll never sleep again," "This will ruin my week") predicts chronic insomnia. Balanced thinking ("This is one difficult night, not a permanent state") allows recovery.

You'll learn specific cognitive techniques for managing racing thoughts in Chapter 8. For now, the key mindset shift is this: acknowledge difficulty without catastrophizing.

Exercise 3: The Worry Dump (10 minutes before bed)

Much of sleep anxiety comes from racing thoughts caused by worries about tomorrow, regrets about today, and our endless mental to-do lists. These thoughts activate your stress response and make sleep physiologically difficult, as we know from Chapter 1 when we talked about the sympathetic nervous system.

The Worry Dump is a simple technique to externalize these thoughts before bed, getting them out of your head and onto paper.

How to do it:

1. About 30-60 minutes before bed, sit down with a notebook or piece of paper.

2. Set a timer for 10 minutes.

3. Write down everything that's on your mind. Don't censor yourself. Don't organize it. Just dump it all out:

- Things you need to do tomorrow
- Worries about work, relationships, health, money
- Things you're annoyed about
- Decisions you need to make
- Anything and everything that's circling in your mind

4. When the timer goes off, stop writing.

5. Look at your list and ask: "Is there anything here that I can actually do something about right now, before bed?"

- If yes, do it (but only if it takes less than 5 minutes).
- If no, write at the bottom: "I'll think about this tomorrow."

6. Close the notebook or fold the paper and put it away, physically and symbolically, setting these worries aside until tomorrow.

Research on cognitive load and pre-sleep worry has shown that writing down concerns before bed significantly reduces the time it takes to fall asleep. A study published in the Journal of Experimental Psychology found that participants who spent 5 minutes writing a to-do list before bed fell asleep an average of 9 minutes faster than those who wrote about completed tasks.

Your brain can stop rehearsing these worries because they're now safely stored on paper. You've acknowledged them, and you've made a plan to address them tomorrow. This allows your mind to let go.

The 80/20 Rule for Sleep

Here's a final principle to embrace: aim for consistency 80% of the time, and give yourself grace for the other 20%.

Sleep advice often presents an all-or-nothing picture: along the lines of 'you must go to bed at exactly the same time every night', 'you must never have caffeine after noon', or 'you must always avoid screens before bed'. This rigidity creates stress and sets you up for feelings of failure.

The reality is that life happens. Sometimes you'll stay up late for a special event. Sometimes you'll have an afternoon coffee because you really need it. Sometimes you'll scroll your phone in bed because you're human and tired and it's comforting. This is normal.

The goal is not perfection, it's consistency. If you follow good sleep practices 80% of the time, you'll see benefits. The occasional deviation won't undo your progress. In fact, being flexible and forgiving with yourself reduces the anxiety that interferes with sleep.

This is the difference between sustainable improvement and exhausting perfectionism. One leads to better sleep. The other leads to burnout and giving up.

How This Looks in Real Life

Let's return to Marcus from the beginning of this chapter. After talking with his doctor, he made some changes, but not the ones he expected.

He didn't buy more sleep gadgets or try harder to optimize his routine. Instead, he deleted his sleep tracking app. He wrote himself a permission slip and put it on his nightstand and he started doing a Worry Dump each evening, getting his racing thoughts out of his head and onto paper. When he found himself lying awake anxiously trying to fall asleep, he practiced paradoxical intention, gently trying to stay awake instead.

Most importantly, he changed his definition of success. Instead of aiming for a perfect sleep score, he aimed for "good enough." He measured success by how he felt and functioned, not by numbers on a screen.

Three weeks later, he reported sleeping better - not perfectly, but noticeably better and he felt less anxious about sleep. The nights when sleep was difficult no longer sent him spiraling into panic because he had learned to let go.

This is the base that everything else builds on. You can learn the most effective breathing techniques, the best relaxation exercises, and the optimal sleep hygiene practices - and we'll cover all of those in the coming chapters. But without this mindset change, those techniques become just another thing to perfect and another performance to stress about.

Sleep is not a test you can fail. It's a natural biological process that happens when you create the right conditions and get out of your own way. Your job is not to force sleep or achieve perfection. Your job is to let go, be kind to yourself, and trust your body to do what it's designed to do.

In the next chapter, we'll build on this foundation with the first practical technique - a simple 10-minute wind-down ritual that signals to your body that it's time to transition from wakefulness to sleep. But you'll do it with the understanding that it's not about doing it perfectly, it's about creating conditions that make sleep more likely, and then letting go of the outcome.

And that's the paradox - the less you try to control sleep, the more it comes naturally.

KEY TAKEAWAYS

Sleep is not a performance. Trying harder activates your stress response, which is incompatible with sleep. The performance paradox means that caring too much about sleeping well makes it harder to actually sleep.

There is no perfect sleep. Everyone experiences night-to-night variability. Normal sleep includes occasional awakenings, lighter nights, and variation in sleep stages. "Good enough" sleep is the goal.

Dysfunctional beliefs maintain insomnia. Catastrophic thinking about sleep, rigid rules about sleep duration, and beliefs about having no control all worsen sleep problems. Identifying and reframing these beliefs is crucial.

Track how you feel, not sleep metrics. Consumer sleep trackers are often inaccurate and create anxiety. Focus on subjective experience and daytime functioning instead.

Paradoxical intention works. Gently trying to stay awake removes performance pressure and allows sleep to happen naturally.

Externalize your worries. The Worry Dump technique gets racing thoughts out of your head and onto paper, reducing cognitive load before bed.

Aim for 80%, not 100%. Consistency most of the time is sufficient. Perfectionism creates stress that interferes with sleep.

Acceptance reduces anxiety. Giving yourself permission to have imperfect sleep, and accepting that some nights will be difficult, paradoxically makes sleep easier.

Before we talk about what you can do in the evening to help you relax and sleep, it's important to begin by mentioning the often forgotten role that the day can have in our sleep patterns and this is covered in the next chapter.

Part 2: The 10-Minute Techniques

Chapter 3

Daytime Habits That Shape Your Night

Jennifer, a 42-year-old marketing director, has the kind of day many poor sleepers will recognize. She does everything she can at night, yet her daytime habits are slowly working against her.

"I do everything right at night," she thinks. "I have blackout curtains, I avoid screens, I do breathing exercises. But I still lie awake for hours. What am I missing?"

Let's take a look at her typical day. She wakes up at 6:30 AM, immediately checks her phone in bed for 20 minutes, then rushes to get ready. She skips breakfast, grabs coffee on the way to work (her first of four cups throughout the day, the last one at 3 PM). Lunch is usually eaten at her desk while working. She sits in meetings or at her computer for most of the day, rarely seeing natural sunlight. After work, she's too tired to exercise. Dinner is often late, around 8:30 PM, and sometimes includes wine to "help her relax." By 10 PM, she's exhausted but wired, unable to sleep despite doing "everything right" at bedtime.

The problem isn't what Jennifer does at night. It's what she does, or doesn't do, during the day.

Your daytime habits profoundly influence your sleep. You can have the perfect nighttime routine, but if your daytime habits work against your biology, sleep will remain elusive.

The good news? Small, strategic changes during the day can have dramatic effects on your nighttime sleep. And true to this book's philosophy, none of these changes require hours of time or perfect execution. We're talking about 10-minute interventions that work with your biology, not against it.

The Morning Light Advantage (10 Minutes That Change Everything)

Let's start with the single most powerful thing you can do for your sleep: get bright light exposure within the first hour of waking up.

Light is the most powerful cue for your body clock. Morning bright light does three crucial things: it suppresses melatonin (preventing grogginess), sets your circadian rhythm (synchronizing your biology with the time of day), and advances your sleep phase (helping you feel sleepy earlier in the evening).

Studies have demonstrated that morning bright light exposure results in higher sleep efficiency, less broken sleep, shorter time in bed, earlier sleep onset, and improved next-day alertness. One study found that just 30 minutes of morning light exposure was sufficient to advance circadian rhythms and improve sleep quality.

How to Get Your Morning Light (10 Minutes)

The goal is simple - get outside within the first hour of waking up, ideally within 30 minutes. Here's how to make it work.

Option 1: The Morning Walk (10 minutes) Step outside and walk around your neighborhood, yard, or even just up and down your driveway. You don't need to exercise vigorously, a gentle stroll is fine. The point is to get your eyes exposed to outdoor light.

Option 2: Coffee or Breakfast Outside (10 minutes) Take your morning coffee or breakfast to a porch, balcony, patio, or park bench. Sit and enjoy it while soaking in the daylight.

Option 3: The Commute Adjustment (10 minutes) If you drive to work, park a 10-minute walk away from your office. If you take public transit, get off one stop early and walk the rest of the way.

Option 4: The Window Strategy (10 minutes, for difficult weather) If it's raining, snowing, or dangerously cold, sit near a window with the curtains open. While this is less effective than being outside, it's better than nothing. Natural light through a window is still significantly brighter than indoor lighting.

Important Details

Don't wear sunglasses during this time. You need the light to reach your eyes to signal your SCN. (Obviously, if it's so bright that it's uncomfortable or unsafe, use sunglasses, but for most morning conditions, you won't need them.)

You don't need direct sunlight. Even on cloudy days, outdoor light is much brighter than indoor lighting. A cloudy day outside provides about 10,000 lux of light, while typical indoor lighting is only 100-500 lux.

Timing matters more than duration. Getting 10 minutes of light within the first hour of waking is more effective than getting 30 minutes at noon. The earlier, the better.

This works year-round. Even in winter, even in northern latitudes, outdoor morning light is beneficial. You might need to stay out a bit longer (15-20 minutes instead of 10), but the principle remains the same.

Timing Is Everything

Caffeine blocks adenosine receptors in your brain, preventing sleepiness. The problem is that it has a much longer effect than most people realize.

Caffeine has a half-life of about 5-6 hours in most people. This means that if you consume 200mg of caffeine (roughly two cups of coffee) at 2 PM, you'll still have about 100mg in your system at 8 PM, and 50mg at 2 AM. That's enough to interfere with sleep, even if you don't consciously feel "wired."

A landmark study examined the effects of caffeine consumed at different times before bed. Researchers found that caffeine consumed even 6 hours before bedtime reduced total sleep time by 41 minutes and significantly disrupted sleep architecture. Participants often didn't realize their sleep had been affected, they fell asleep eventually, but objective measurements showed reduced sleep quality and efficiency.

A comprehensive systematic review analyzing multiple studies found that caffeine consumption reduced total sleep time by an average of 45 minutes, decreased sleep efficiency by 7%, increased the time it took to fall asleep by 9 minutes, and increased nighttime awakenings. These effects were dose-dependent: the more caffeine consumed, the worse the impact.

The Strategic Caffeine Cut-Off (Takes 0 Minutes, Saves Hours of Sleep)

The rule you should follow is to have no caffeine after 2 PM. For most people, this allows enough time for caffeine to clear your system before bedtime.

However, individuals are different and some people metabolize caffeine faster due to genetic differences, while others metabolize it more slowly (for example, older adults tend to metabolize caffeine more slowly than younger adults). If you're particularly sensitive to caffeine, you might need to cut it off even earlier. sometimes noon or even late morning.

How do you know if caffeine is affecting your sleep? Try an experiment. For two weeks, cut off all caffeine by noon and track how you feel, and how you sleep using the "Good Enough" sleep log from Chapter 2. Then, for the next two weeks, allow yourself afternoon caffeine. Compare the results. Your own experience is the best guide.

What Counts as Caffeine?

Don't just think about coffee. Caffeine is also in:

- Tea (black, green, white, oolong): 25-50mg per cup
- Energy drinks: 80-300mg per serving
- Soda: 30-50mg per can
- Chocolate: 10-30mg per ounce (dark chocolate has more)
- Some medications: headache pills, cold remedies, weight loss supplements

Even decaf coffee isn't completely caffeine-free. It can contain 2-5mg per cup, which is negligible for most people but worth knowing if you're extremely sensitive.

The Morning Caffeine Strategy

Interestingly, delaying your first cup of coffee by 90-120 minutes after waking can actually make caffeine more effective.

This is because cortisol, your body's natural alertness hormone, peaks shortly after waking. Consuming caffeine during this natural cortisol spike doesn't add much benefit because you're already alert. But as cortisol begins to decline mid-morning, that's when caffeine can provide the most noticeable boost.

So instead of reaching for coffee the moment you wake up, try to get your morning light exposure first, let your natural cortisol do its job, and have your coffee around 9 or 10 AM. You might even find that it's more effective, and you won't build tolerance as quickly.

Why Your Nightcap Backfires

Many people use alcohol as a sleep aid. This makes sense on the surface. Alcohol is a sedative, it makes you feel relaxed and drowsy, and it can help you fall asleep faster. The problem is what happens after you fall asleep.

Alcohol fundamentally disrupts sleep architecture. Research consistently shows that alcohol consumption before bed produces a pattern of increased slow-wave sleep (deep sleep) in the first half of the night, followed by significant disruption in the second half. Specifically, alcohol suppresses REM sleep early in the night, and as your body metabolizes the alcohol, you experience a "REM rebound" that causes frequent awakenings, lighter sleep, and vivid or disturbing dreams.

A systematic review examining the effects of alcohol on sleep found that even moderate alcohol consumption (equivalent to 1-2 drinks) caused a delay in REM sleep onset and a reduction in total REM sleep duration. Sleep became more fragmented, with more frequent awakenings in the second half of the night. Participants often reported feeling unrefreshed in the morning despite having "slept" for a full night.

The effect is dose-dependent: the more you drink, the worse the disruption. But even small amounts can affect sleep quality, particularly in older adults who metabolize alcohol more slowly.

The Practical Ways to Manage Alcohol and Sleep

I'm not going to tell you never to drink alcohol, that's not realistic for most people, and it violates the 80/20 principle we discussed in Chapter 2. But if sleep is a priority, here are evidence-based guidelines:

1. Avoid alcohol within 3-4 hours of bedtime. If you're going to drink, do it earlier in the evening to give your body time to metabolize it before sleep.
2. Limit quantity. One drink is less disruptive than three. If you're going to drink, keep it moderate.
3. Don't use alcohol as a sleep aid. If you find yourself regularly relying on alcohol to fall asleep, that's a sign of a deeper sleep problem that needs to be addressed with the techniques in this book, not masked with sedation.
4. Hydrate. Alcohol is dehydrating, which can cause nighttime awakenings. If you do drink, have water alongside it and before bed.
5. Pay attention to your own response. Some people are more sensitive to alcohol's sleep-disrupting effects than others. Use your "Good Enough" sleep log to track how you sleep on nights when you drink versus nights when you don't.

Movement, Exercise and Sleep

The relationship between exercise and sleep is bidirectional and powerful. Good sleep improves exercise performance and recovery. Regular exercise improves sleep quality, reduces the time it takes to fall asleep, and increases the amount of deep sleep you get. It's one of the most well-established non-pharmacological interventions for insomnia.

A systematic review analyzing multiple studies found that people who exercised regularly fell asleep faster, slept longer, and reported better sleep quality compared to sedentary individuals. Another meta-analysis found that exercise training resulted in significant improvements in subjective sleep quality, particularly in middle-aged and older adults.

There are multiple reasons why this can help. Exercise increases sleep pressure by increasing adenosine buildup (remember from Chapter 1, more adenosine means more sleep drive). It reduces anxiety and depression, both of which interfere with sleep. It helps regulate circadian rhythms, particularly when done outdoors in natural light. It raises body temperature during the workout, and the subsequent drop in temperature several hours later promotes sleepiness.

The Exercise Timing Question

For decades, conventional wisdom said "don't exercise close to bedtime because it will keep you awake." Recent research has challenged this assumption. Multiple studies have found that moderate evening exercise does not negatively affect sleep and may actually improve it for many people.

A 2023 review examining exercise timing found that short-term evening exercise and even high-intensity exercise did not have significant negative effects on sleep quality for most people. In fact, some participants experienced improved sleep.

However, and this is important, there's significant individual variation. Some people find that vigorous exercise within 2-3 hours of bedtime leaves them too energized to sleep. Others have no problem. A recent dose-response study found that to optimize sleep timing, duration, and quality, individuals should ideally stop exercising four or more hours before bedtime, but acknowledged that this varies by person.

Just experiment and find what works for you. Don't avoid exercise altogether because you can only fit it in during the evening - evening exercise is far better than no exercise. But if you notice it affects your sleep, try to finish at least 2-3 hours before bedtime, or switch to gentler forms of movement in the evening (walking, yoga, stretching) and save vigorous workouts for earlier in the day.

The 10-Minute Movement Prescription

You don't need to run marathons or spend hours in the gym to see sleep benefits. Research shows that even moderate physical activity improves sleep. Here are practical 10-minute options:

Morning: The Wake-Up Walk (10 minutes) This combines two powerful interventions: morning light exposure and movement. Take a brisk 10-minute walk outside within an hour of waking. You're building sleep pressure for tonight while simultaneously setting your circadian clock.

Midday: The Movement Break (10 minutes) If you have a sedentary job, set a timer to get up and move every 2-3 hours. Walk around the building, do some stretches, climb stairs, do anything that gets your body moving. This prevents the sluggishness that comes from prolonged sitting and helps maintain healthy sleep pressure.

Evening: The Wind-Down Walk (10 minutes) A gentle walk after dinner aids digestion, provides light movement, and can be part of your transition from daytime activity to evening relaxation. Keep it gentle, this isn't a workout, it's a wind-down.

Consistency Over Intensity Ten minutes of daily movement is more beneficial for sleep than an intense 90-minute workout once a week. Aim for regular, moderate activity rather than sporadic intense exercise.

Is Napping Friend or Foe?

Napping is a controversial topic when it comes to insomnia. For some people, a strategic nap can be refreshing and helpful. For others, particularly those struggling with nighttime sleep, napping can make insomnia worse.

Here's what you need to know.

Why Napping Can Worsen Nighttime Insomnia

Sleep pressure builds the longer you're awake. When you nap during the day, you release some of that pressure, leaving less built up for bedtime. This makes it harder to fall asleep and stay asleep at night.

For people who already struggle with insomnia, this can create a vicious cycle:

1. You sleep poorly at night
2. You feel exhausted during the day
3. You nap to cope with the exhaustion
4. The nap reduces your sleep pressure
5. You have even more difficulty sleeping that night
6. The cycle repeats

Research on CBT-I (Cognitive Behavioral Therapy for Insomnia) typically recommends eliminating daytime napping for people with chronic insomnia, at least initially. Multiple studies have shown that avoiding naps helps consolidate nighttime sleep.

When Napping Is Okay

That said, napping isn't always bad. Strategic napping can be appropriate in certain situations:

Short naps (20 minutes or less): Brief naps that don't enter deep sleep stages have minimal impact on nighttime sleep pressure. These "power naps" can provide a boost of alertness without significantly affecting your ability to sleep at night.

Napping earlier in the day: A nap in the early afternoon before 2 PM gives your body more time to rebuild sleep pressure before bedtime. A nap at 1 PM has less impact on a 10 PM bedtime than a nap at 5 PM.

Occasional, not habitual: An occasional nap when you're genuinely exhausted or ill is different from daily habitual napping. If you slept terribly last night and have an important meeting this afternoon, a brief nap might be appropriate.

When you're a good nighttime sleeper: If you don't have insomnia and sleep well at night, moderate napping probably won't cause problems. Some people can nap regularly without affecting their nighttime sleep.

Special Situations

Shift workers

If you work night shifts or rotating shifts, strategic napping is often necessary and beneficial. The rules are different when your sleep schedule doesn't align with normal circadian patterns.

Illness or recovery

When you're sick or recovering from illness, your body needs extra rest. Napping during illness is appropriate and helpful.

Temporary sleep deprivation

If you've had several nights of very poor sleep due to a crisis situation, a nap might be necessary for safety and function. This is different from chronic insomnia.

Pregnancy

Increased fatigue during pregnancy often necessitates napping. This is a temporary phase.

Should You Nap?

If you have chronic insomnia (difficulty falling asleep or staying asleep most nights), try eliminating naps for 2-4 weeks while implementing the other techniques in this book. See if your nighttime sleep improves.

If you occasionally nap, keep them short (20 minutes maximum) and early (before 2 PM). Set an alarm so you don't accidentally sleep longer.

If you feel you must nap, ask yourself: Am I genuinely exhausted and unable to function safely? Or am I napping out of habit or boredom? If it's the latter, try replacing the nap with a different activity: a short walk, some stretching, a change of scenery, or a brief social interaction.

Track the connection: Use your sleep log (from Chapter 11) to track whether napping affects your nighttime sleep. On days you nap, do you have more difficulty falling asleep or staying asleep that night? This personal data will guide your decision.

How to Eliminate Napping If Needed

If you decide to stop napping to improve nighttime sleep, here's how to manage the change. But remember that the first few days without naps can be difficult. You'll feel tired. This is temporary. Your body will adjust and consolidate your sleep at night.

Use the 10-minute strategies from this chapter

When you feel the urge to nap, take a 10-minute walk instead, get some sunlight, drink water, do some gentle stretches, or change your environment. Often the urge to nap will pass.

Avoid caffeine as a substitute

Don't start drinking extra coffee to compensate for eliminating naps. This will backfire and worsen your nighttime sleep.

Go to bed slightly earlier temporarily

If you're eliminating a daily nap, you might need to move your bedtime 30 minutes earlier for the first week or two while your body adjusts.

Be patient

It typically takes 1-2 weeks for your nighttime sleep to improve after eliminating daytime naps. Don't give up after three days.

The Bottom Line on Napping

For most people with insomnia, avoiding naps (or limiting them to brief, early afternoon power naps) helps consolidate nighttime sleep. The temporary daytime fatigue you experience when you stop napping will actually help you sleep better at night by increasing sleep pressure.

If you're a good nighttime sleeper, moderate napping is fine. But if you struggle with insomnia, napping is likely making it worse.

The Food-Sleep Connection

The relationship between diet and sleep is complex and still being researched, but some clear patterns have emerged. Overall dietary patterns matter more than individual foods, but timing and composition of meals, particularly your last meal of the day, can significantly affect sleep.

Dietary Patterns and Sleep Quality

Research examining the association between diet and sleep quality found that healthy food consumption (fruits, vegetables, whole grains, lean proteins) was associated with better sleep, while processed foods and foods high in added sugars were linked to worse sleep features.

Specifically, research has shown the following:

High-fiber diets are associated with more deep, restorative slow-wave sleep. A controlled feeding study found that higher fiber intake predicted more time in deep sleep, while higher saturated fat and sugar intake predicted lighter, more disrupted sleep.

Mediterranean-style diets (rich in fruits, vegetables, whole grains, fish, olive oil, and nuts) have been associated with better sleep quality in multiple studies.

Diets high in processed foods, refined carbohydrates, and added sugars are associated with more disrupted sleep, less deep sleep, and more nighttime awakenings.

The mechanisms aren't fully understood, but likely involve inflammation, blood sugar regulation, gut microbiome effects, and nutrient availability for neurotransmitter production.

The Timing of Your Last Meal

Eating a large meal close to bedtime can interfere with sleep in a number of ways. Digestion requires energy and increases body temperature, both of which are incompatible with sleep. Lying down with a full stomach can cause acid reflux, which disrupts sleep. Large meals late at night can also affect circadian rhythms and metabolic processes.

Research suggests finishing your last substantial meal at least 3-4 hours before bedtime. This gives your body time to digest before you lie down. If you need a small snack closer to bedtime, choose something light and easy to digest.

Specific Foods and Sleep

While overall dietary patterns matter most, some specific foods have been studied for their effects on sleep:

Tart cherry juice contains natural melatonin and has been shown in small studies to modestly improve sleep duration and quality. However, the effect is small, and drinking large amounts of any liquid close to bedtime can cause nighttime bathroom trips.

Kiwifruit has been associated with improved sleep onset and duration in a few small studies, possibly due to its serotonin content and antioxidants.

Fatty fish (salmon, mackerel, sardines) are rich in omega-3 fatty acids and vitamin D, both of which have been linked to better sleep quality in observational studies.

Warm milk has a long-standing reputation as a sleep aid. The evidence is mixed. Milk contains tryptophan, an amino acid precursor to serotonin and melatonin, but the amounts are small. The benefit may be more psychological (a comforting bedtime ritual) than physiological, but if it works for you, that's what matters.

Foods to avoid close to bedtime: Spicy foods (can cause heartburn), high-fat foods (slow digestion), large amounts of protein (can be stimulating), and anything that causes you personally to have digestive discomfort.

The 10-Minute Meal Planning Strategy

Rather than obsessing over specific "sleep foods," focus on overall patterns:

1. Eat regular meals at consistent times. This helps regulate your circadian rhythm. Your body expects food at certain times, and irregular eating can disrupt your internal clock.
2. Front-load your calories. Eat a substantial breakfast and lunch, and a lighter dinner. This balances with your circadian rhythm and your metabolism is more efficient earlier in the day.
3. Finish dinner 3-4 hours before bed. If you eat dinner at 6 PM and go to bed at 10 PM, you've given your body time to digest.
4. If you need an evening snack, keep it small and balanced. A small serving of complex carbohydrates with a bit of protein (like whole grain crackers with cheese, or a small bowl of oatmeal) is less likely to disrupt sleep than a large, heavy snack.
5. Stay hydrated during the day, but remember that drinking large amounts of water right before bed increases the likelihood of nighttime bathroom trips. Sip water throughout the day, and reduce intake in the 1-2 hours before bed.

A Sample Day

Let's redesign Jennifer's day using these principles:

6:30 AM - Wake up: Instead of immediately checking her phone, Jennifer gets out of bed and opens the curtains.

6:45 AM - Morning light + movement (10 minutes): She takes a 10-

minute walk around the block, getting morning light exposure and gentle movement.

7:00 AM - Breakfast: She eats a balanced breakfast at home, something with protein, healthy fats, and complex carbs to stabilize blood sugar.

9:00 AM - First coffee: She waits until mid-morning for her first cup of coffee, when her natural cortisol has started to decline.

12:00 PM - Lunch + light: She eats lunch away from her desk, ideally near a window or, better yet, outside if weather permits.

2:00 PM - Last caffeine: Her final cup of coffee or tea is finished by 2 PM, giving her body 8+ hours to metabolize it before bed.

3:00 PM - Movement break (10 minutes): She sets a timer and takes a quick walk or does some stretching.

6:00 PM - Dinner: She eats a moderate dinner with her family, finishing by 6:30 PM.

7:30 PM - Evening walk (10 minutes): A gentle stroll around the neighborhood to aid digestion and begin the transition to evening.

8:00 PM - Wind-down begins: No more work emails, no more stimulating activities. She might read, do a puzzle, or have a relaxed conversation.

10:00 PM - Bedtime: She's given her body 3.5 hours to digest dinner, 8 hours to clear caffeine, and she's built appropriate sleep pressure through morning movement and light exposure.

Notice what changed, Jennifer didn't add hours to her day. She made strategic 10-minute adjustments that work with her biology instead of against it. The morning walk replaced her 20 minutes of phone scrolling. The movement breaks took time she was already spending at work. The evening walk replaced time she would have spent watching TV.

The 80/20 Principle Applies Here Too

As we discussed in Chapter 2, perfection is not the goal. You don't need to execute all of these strategies perfectly every single day. Life happens. Sometimes you'll have afternoon coffee because you really need it. Sometimes you'll eat dinner late because of a special event. Sometimes you'll skip your morning walk because you're running late.

That's okay. Aim for consistency 80% of the time. The goal is to establish patterns that generally support your sleep, not to create rigid rules that add stress to your life.

If you can implement just two or three of these strategies consistently, say, morning light exposure, a caffeine cut-off, and regular movement, you'll likely see significant improvements in your sleep. You don't have to do everything at once. Start with what feels most doable, establish that habit, and then add another.

What You Need to Remember

Your daytime habits profoundly affect your nighttime sleep. No amount of perfect bedtime routine can compensate for a day spent working against your biology.

Morning light exposure (10 minutes within an hour of waking) is the single most powerful circadian intervention you can make. It sets your internal clock, suppresses daytime melatonin, and promotes alertness.

Caffeine has a 5-6 hour half-life. Cut it off by 2 PM (or earlier if you're sensitive) to prevent it from interfering with sleep.

Alcohol disrupts sleep architecture, particularly REM sleep and sleep in the second half of the night. Avoid it within 3-4 hours of bedtime.

Regular movement improves sleep quality and increases deep sleep. Even 10 minutes of daily activity helps. Exercise timing varies by individual, experiment to find what works for you.

Overall dietary patterns matter more than specific foods. Focus on whole foods, adequate fiber, and regular meal timing. Finish your last substantial meal 3-4 hours before bed.

Consistency beats perfection. Implement these strategies 80% of the time and you'll see benefits. Don't let the pursuit of perfect daytime habits become another source of stress.

In the next chapter, we'll build on this foundation with your first nighttime technique - the 10-minute wind-down ritual that signals to your body it's time to transition from wakefulness to sleep. But now you understand that what happens during the day is just as important as what happens at night.

Chapter 4

The 10-Minute Wind-Down Ritual

Rachel checks the time on her phone: 10:47 PM. She has been scrolling through social media for the past hour, telling herself she'll go to bed "in just a few more minutes."

Her eyes feel tired, but her mind is buzzing with information from news updates, friends' vacation photos, work emails that popped up in her notifications.

Finally, at 11:15 PM, she puts down her phone, brushes her teeth, and gets into bed. She turns off the light and... nothing. Despite feeling exhausted moments ago, she's now wide awake, her mind racing through everything she just saw on her phone, plus tomorrow's to-do list, plus that awkward conversation from three days ago that her brain has decided to replay in vivid detail.

Sound familiar?

Rachel's problem isn't that she's not tired enough. Her problem is that she's asking her body to go from 60 miles per hour to zero in an instant. She's expecting her brain to move from full alertness, stimulated by bright screens, engaging content, and the mild stress of work emails, directly into sleep mode. That's not how human biology works.

As we know, sleep happens when your body moves from stress mode to relaxation mode. This transition doesn't happen instantaneously. Your body needs a signal, a transition period, a bridge between wakefulness and sleep. That's what a wind-down ritual provides.

THE SCIENCE OF ROUTINES AND SLEEP

Humans are creatures of habit. Our brains love patterns and predictability. When you do the same sequence of actions at the same time each night, your brain begins to associate those actions with sleep. This is called classical conditioning, and it's one of the most powerful tools in behavioral sleep medicine.

Think about Pavlov's dogs, which learned to salivate at the sound of a bell because it had been repeatedly paired with food. Your brain can learn the same way because when you consistently perform certain calming activities before bed, your brain begins to initiate the sleep process as soon as those activities start. It means that the routine itself becomes a cue for sleep.

This principle is formalized in Cognitive Behavioral Therapy for Insomnia (CBT-I) as stimulus control therapy. The goal is to strengthen the association between your bed, your bedroom, and sleep, while weakening the association between your bed and wakefulness, worry, or stimulating activities. Research on stimulus control has shown it to be one of the most effective components of CBT-I, significantly reducing the time it takes to fall asleep and improving overall sleep quality.

Studies examining bedtime routines have found consistent benefits. Research with adults has shown that having a regular bedtime routine is associated with earlier bedtimes, shorter time to fall asleep, better sleep quality, and reduced bedtime anxiety. A systematic review examining sleep hygiene practices found that consistent bedtime routines were one of the most strongly associated factors with good sleep quality.

The routine doesn't have to be complicated. In fact, simpler is often better. All that matters is consistency and the intentional mental change from activity to calm.

THE CORE PRINCIPLES OF AN EFFECTIVE WIND-DOWN

Before we get into the specific 10-minute sequence, let's establish the principles that make a wind-down routine effective:

1. Consistency in Timing

Your routine should start at roughly the same time each night, ideally 30-60 minutes before your target bedtime. This regularity helps set your circadian rhythm, as we discussed in Chapter 3. Your body begins to anticipate sleep at this time, releasing melatonin and lowering body temperature in preparation.

Does this mean you can never vary your bedtime? No. Remember the 80/20 principle from Chapter 2. Aim for consistency most nights, and don't stress about occasional variations for social events or special circumstances.

2. Gradual Reduction of Stimulation

Your routine should progressively reduce sensory input and cognitive engagement. You're creating a gentle slope from wakefulness to sleep, not a cliff. This means:

- Dimming lights gradually (we'll discuss this more below)
- Reducing noise or transitioning to calming sounds

- Shifting from engaging activities (work, intense conversations, stimulating entertainment) to passive, calming ones
- Slowing your physical movements from daytime pace to evening ease

3. Separation from Stress and Work

Your wind-down time is when you stop engaging with anything that could trigger your stress response. This means:

- No work emails or tasks
- No difficult conversations or problem-solving
- No checking news or social media (both are designed to be stimulating and often stressful)
- No paying bills or dealing with logistics

These activities activate your sympathetic nervous system, the opposite of what you need for sleep. They can wait until tomorrow.

4. Association with Your Sleep Space

The final part of your routine should happen in or near your bedroom, helping your brain associate this space with the transition to sleep. However, you should not get into bed until you're actually ready to sleep. This is a key principle of stimulus control: the bed should be strongly associated with sleep (and sex), not with other activities.

5. Personalization Within Structure

While I'll give you a template, your routine should include activities that you personally find calming. What relaxes one person might bore or irritate another. The structure is consistent (dim lights, reduce stimulation, calm activities), but the specific content can be tailored to your preferences.

The Basic 10-Minute Wind-Down Sequence

Here's a simple, effective template you can start with tonight. Think of this as your foundation which you can modify as you learn what works best for you.

Minutes 1-2: The Transition Signal

What to do: Dim the lights throughout your home and put away all screens (phone, tablet, computer, TV). If you must check your phone one last time, do it now, then put it in another room or at least across the room from your bed.

Why it works: Bright light, especially the blue wavelengths emitted by screens, suppresses melatonin production and signals to your brain that it's still daytime. Dimming lights and removing screens removes this signal, allowing melatonin to rise naturally.

Research has consistently shown that evening exposure to bright light and screens delays circadian rhythms and makes it harder to fall asleep. One study found that using electronic devices before bed delayed melatonin onset by an average of 1.5 hours. Conversely, reducing light exposure in the evening promotes earlier melatonin release and sleepiness.

Practical tips

- Use lamps instead of overhead lights in the evening
- Consider warm-toned bulbs (amber or red-shifted light is less disruptive than blue-white light)
- If you need to use screens in the evening, enable "night mode" or blue light filters, though complete avoidance is better
- Set your phone to "Do Not Disturb" mode so you're not tempted by notifications

What if I need to check my phone?: If you absolutely must check your phone for an urgent message or set an alarm, do it during these first two minutes, then commit to putting it away, and make this the exception, not the rule.

Minutes 3-5: Gentle Physical Activity

What to do: Engage in light, calming movement. Options include:

- Gentle stretching: Focus on areas that hold tension. The neck, shoulders, hips, lower back. Move slowly and breathe deeply. This isn't a workout; it's a release.
- Slow walking: A brief, leisurely walk around your home or outside (if safe and weather permits). Keep the pace slow and meditative.
- Restorative yoga poses: Simple poses like child's pose, legs-up-the-wall, or gentle twists. Hold each for 30-60 seconds, breathing slowly.

Why it works: Gentle movement helps release physical tension accumulated during the day. It also provides a kinesthetic signal that you're transitioning from activity to rest. The key word is "gentle" because vigorous exercise would be counterproductive, as it would raise your heart rate and body temperature, both of which interfere with sleep.

Additionally, focusing on physical sensations during stretching or slow movement helps redirect attention away from racing thoughts. You're grounding yourself in your body rather than staying stuck in your mind.

Practical tips:

- Keep movements slow and deliberate
- Breathe deeply and naturally as you move
- Pay attention to how your body feels and notice areas of tension and consciously relax them
- If you're not flexible or have physical limitations, modify as needed; the goal is gentle release, not perfect form

What if I'm too tired to move? That's fine. Skip this part and move directly to the relaxation technique. The routine is flexible, so use what serves you on any given night.

Minutes 6-10: Relaxation Technique

What to do: Practice one of the relaxation techniques we'll cover in detail in the next few chapters. For now, here's a simple option to get you started:

The 4-7-8 Breathing Technique (we'll explore this more deeply in Chapter 5):

1. Sit or lie in a comfortable position
2. Place the tip of your tongue against the ridge behind your upper front teeth (this is optional but traditional)
3. Exhale completely through your mouth, making a "whoosh" sound

4. Close your mouth and inhale quietly through your nose for a count of 4
5. Hold your breath for a count of 7
6. Exhale completely through your mouth for a count of 8, making a "whoosh" sound
7. Repeat this cycle 3-4 times

As we discussed in Chapter 1, controlled breathing activates your relaxation response. The 4-7-8 pattern specifically emphasizes the exhale, which is associated with relaxation. The counting gives your mind something neutral to focus on, preventing it from wandering to stressful thoughts.

Research on breathing exercises has shown they reduce heart rate, lower blood pressure, decrease anxiety, and promote the physiological state conducive to sleep. The 4-7-8 technique specifically has been studied for its effects on reducing anxiety and encouraging relaxation.

Alternative options (we'll cover these in depth in later chapters):

- Body scan meditation (Chapter 6): Systematically relax each part of your body
- Progressive muscle relaxation (Chapter 7): Tense and release muscle groups
- Visualization (Chapter 8): Imagine a peaceful, calming scene in detail

Ideally you will choose one technique and practice it consistently because it means your brain will learn to associate this technique with the transition to sleep.

Practical tips:

- Start with just 3-4 breath cycles; you can extend this as you get comfortable

- If counting feels stressful, just focus on making your exhale longer than your inhale
- It's normal for your mind to wander; gently bring it back to your breath
- You can do this sitting up or lying in bed (if you're ready to sleep)

After the 10 Minutes: To Bed (or Not)

There is a crucial principle from stimulus control therapy which says you should only get into bed when you're actually sleepy.

Sleepy means your eyes feel heavy, you're yawning, your body feels ready to lie down and drift off. Sleepy is different from tired. You can be exhausted (tired) but not sleepy - your body is fatigued but your brain is still alert. If you get into bed when you're tired but not sleepy, you'll lie there awake, which strengthens the association between your bed and wakefulness. That's the opposite of what you want.

So after your 10-minute wind-down:-

If you feel sleepy then go to bed. Turn off the light. If you're not asleep within about 10-15 minutes, get up and do something boring in dim light until you feel sleepy again (we'll cover this more in Chapter 10 when we take a look at middle-of-the-night awakenings).

If you don't feel sleepy yet that's okay too. Do something quiet and boring in dim light. Read a book (not on a screen), do a puzzle, listen to calm music, fold laundry. Avoid anything stimulating. When you start to feel sleepy, then go to bed.

This might feel counterintuitive. You might think, "But I need to go to bed at 10 PM to get 8 hours of sleep!" Remember from Chapter 2: trying to force sleep doesn't work (and it can still be restorative without being perfect). It's better to go to bed at 10:30 PM when you're actually sleepy and fall asleep quickly than to go to bed at 10 PM and lie awake for an hour.

PERSONALIZING YOUR ROUTINE

The 10-minute template above is a starting point which you can personalize - here are some examples.

Choose Your Calming Activities

The "gentle physical activity" and "relaxation technique" components can be customized based on what you find genuinely calming. Some options:

Physical options:

- Gentle stretching or yoga
- Slow walking
- Self-massage (neck, shoulders, feet)
- Taking a warm bath or shower (the subsequent drop in body temperature promotes sleepiness)
- Preparing your bedroom (fluffing pillows, adjusting temperature)

Relaxation technique options (more detail in upcoming chapters):

- Breathing exercises
- Body scan meditation
- Progressive muscle relaxation
- Guided imagery/visualization
- Listening to calming music or nature sounds
- Gentle reading (physical books, not screens)
- Journaling (the "worry dump" from Chapter 2)

What to avoid:

- Anything that requires bright light
- Anything cognitively engaging or stimulating (exciting books, puzzles that frustrate you, planning or problem-solving)
- Anything that could trigger stress or strong emotions
- Anything involving screens (TV, phone, computer, tablet)

Adjust the Timing

While 10 minutes is the minimum effective wind-down, some people benefit from a longer period from 15, 20, or even 30 minutes. Find out what works for you and make sure that it's long enough to actually move your physiology from alert to calm. But don't make it so long that it becomes burdensome because this could cause you to lose the motivation and the consistency.

If you're someone who takes a long time to wind down, you might structure it like this:

- 30 minutes before bed: Stop all work and screens, dim lights
- 20 minutes before bed: Gentle activity (bath, stretching, reading)
- 10 minutes before bed: Relaxation technique (breathing, body scan)
- Bedtime: Get into bed only when sleepy

Adapt for Your Living Situation

If you have a partner with a different schedule: Use headphones for guided meditations or calming music. Do your stretching or reading in another room if needed. Communicate with your partner about the importance of your wind-down time.

If you have young children: Your wind-down might happen after you've put them to bed. If they wake up during your routine, tend to them, then resume where you left off. Be flexible, some nights won't be perfect, and that's okay (80/20 principle).

If you work night shifts or have an irregular schedule: The principles still apply, but you'll need to adapt the timing. Your "evening" is whenever you're preparing for your main sleep period, regardless of the clock time. It is all about consistency relative to your sleep schedule, not to the sun.

If you live in a noisy environment: Use earplugs, white noise machines, or calming music through headphones to create your own sound environment during your wind-down.

Common Obstacles and Solutions

"I don't have time for a wind-down routine"

You're already spending time getting to sleep, you might simply be doing it inefficiently. Scrolling your phone for 30 minutes before bed isn't saving time; it's making sleep harder, which costs you time lying awake. Ten minutes of intentional wind-down is more efficient than 30-60 minutes of lying in bed unable to sleep.

Also, remember that you can combine activities. If you need to do certain tasks in the evening (like preparing tomorrow's lunch or tidying up), do them during the early part of your wind-down with dimmed lights and a calm mindset. It's the quality of the activity that matters here, you are not aiming to add extra time.

"My mind races no matter what I do"

This is where the cognitive techniques from Chapter 2 come in. Do a "worry dump" as part of your wind-down and write down everything on your mind, then close the notebook. Practice the cognitive reframing we discussed: "These thoughts can wait until tomorrow. Right now is for rest."

If racing thoughts persist, it may be a sign that you need more practice with the relaxation techniques (breathing, body scan, etc.) that we'll cover in the next chapters. These techniques specifically target the racing mind.

"I fall asleep on the couch but then can't sleep in bed"

This is a common stimulus control issue. You've accidentally trained your brain to associate the couch with sleep and the bed with wakefulness. The solution: when you start feeling sleepy on the couch during your wind-down, immediately go to bed. Don't wait until you're fully asleep. You want to transfer that sleepiness to your bed, strengthening the bed-sleep association.

"My partner wants to watch TV or use their phone in bed"

This is a conversation about boundaries and priorities. Explain that you're working on improving your sleep and need the bedroom to be a calm, dark space during your wind-down and sleep time. Ask if they'd be willing to use headphones, or to watch TV in another room if possible. If that's not feasible, consider using an eye mask and earplugs to create your own environment.

"I feel silly doing a 'routine' like I'm a child"

Reframe this because you're not being childish, you're being strategic. Elite athletes have pre-performance routines. Surgeons have pre-surgery routines. Pilots have pre-flight checklists. These aren't childish, they're professional tools that ensure consistency and optimal performance. Your wind-down routine is the same: a tool that ensures your brain and body are prepared for high-quality sleep.

The First Week: What to Expect

When you start implementing a wind-down routine, don't expect immediate perfection. Your brain needs time to learn the new association between these activities and sleep. Here's what's realistic:

Night 1-3: The routine might feel awkward or forced. You might not notice immediate improvements in sleep. That's normal. You're establishing a new pattern, and your brain hasn't learned it yet. Focus on consistency, not results.

Night 4-7: You'll likely start noticing that the routine itself feels calming, even if sleep hasn't dramatically improved yet. Your body is beginning to recognize the pattern.

Week 2-3: Most people start seeing noticeable improvements in how quickly they fall asleep and how calm they feel at bedtime. The routine starts to feel natural rather than forced.

Week 4+: The routine becomes automatic. Your body begins to initiate the sleep process as soon as you start the routine. You've successfully conditioned a new response.

Remember from Chapter 2: measure success by how you feel, not by perfect execution. Some nights you'll do the full routine. Some nights you'll do an abbreviated version. Some nights you'll skip it entirely due to circumstances. That's life. The goal is consistency most of the time, not perfection all the time.

How This Looks

Let's revisit Rachel from the beginning of this chapter. Here's what her evening looks like now:

9:30 PM: She finishes her last work task and closes her laptop. She does a quick "worry dump," writing down anything on her mind for tomorrow.

10:00 PM: She dims the lights throughout her apartment. She checks her phone one last time, sets it to "Do Not Disturb," and plugs it in to charge in the kitchen, not her bedroom.

10:05 PM: She does 3-4 minutes of gentle stretching in her living room, focusing on her neck and shoulders where she holds tension. She moves slowly, breathing deeply.

10:10 PM: She sits in her dimly lit bedroom and practices 4-7-8 breathing for 4 cycles (about 4 minutes). Her mind wanders a few times, but she gently brings it back to counting.

10:15 PM: She brushes her teeth, washes her face, and gets into comfortable pajamas.

10:20 PM: She feels sleepy, her eyes are heavy, she's yawning. She gets into bed, turns off the light, and falls asleep within about 10 minutes.

Total time: 20 minutes from starting her wind-down to being in bed, 10 minutes of which was the core routine. She's asleep by 10:30 PM instead of lying awake until midnight like she used to.

The difference? She gave her body the time it needed. She worked with her biology instead of against it.

Before You Move On

A wind-down routine is a bridge between wakefulness and sleep. Your body cannot transition instantly from full alertness to sleep. It needs a signal and a gradual reduction in stimulation.

Consistency is more important than perfection. Do your routine at roughly the same time each night, using the same sequence of activities. Your brain will learn to associate these activities with sleep.

The core components are: dim lights and remove screens (minutes 1-2), gentle physical activity (minutes 3-5), and a relaxation technique (minutes 6-10).

Only get into bed when you're actually sleepy, not just tired. This strengthens the association between your bed and sleep.

Customize within the structure. Choose calming activities that you personally find relaxing, but maintain the overall pattern of reducing stimulation.

Give it time. Your brain needs 1-3 weeks to learn the new pattern. Don't judge the routine's effectiveness after just one or two nights.

The routine itself becomes a cue for sleep. Through classical conditioning, your brain will begin to initiate the sleep process as soon as you start your routine.

In the next chapter, we'll cover the first relaxation technique: breathing exercises. You'll learn multiple evidence-based breathing patterns that activate your relaxation response and prepare your body for sleep. These will become the core of your wind-down routine's final 5-10 minutes.

Chapter 5

Breathe Your Way to Sleep

Now let's meet Tom who is lying in bed, eyes wide open, mind racing. He's thinking about tomorrow's presentation, the email he forgot to send, and if he remembered to lock the back door. His heart is beating faster than it should. His jaw is clenched. His shoulders are up near his ears. He knows he needs to relax, but he doesn't know how. His body seems to have forgotten how to calm down.

What Tom doesn't realize is that he has a built-in relaxation tool that he's been using his entire life, but never consciously controlled - his breath.

Your breath is the most accessible tool you have for influencing your nervous system. As we learned earlier, sleep happens when your parasympathetic nervous system - the "rest and digest" system- takes over from your sympathetic nervous system (the "fight or flight" system). While you can't directly command your nervous system to switch modes, you can use your breath as a bridge between conscious control and automatic physiological response.

This chapter will teach you three evidence-based breathing techniques that take 5-10 minutes and can be practiced anywhere, anytime. You'll learn exactly how to do each one, when to use which technique, and what the science says about why they work. By the end of this chapter, you'll have powerful, portable tools that you can use during your wind-down routine (from Chapter 4) or anytime you need to shift from stress to calm.

Why Breathing Works: The Science

Before we talk about the techniques, let's understand why something as simple as changing your breathing pattern can have such profound effects on your ability to sleep.

The Vagus Nerve Connection

Your vagus nerve is the longest nerve in your body, running from your brainstem down through your chest and abdomen. It's the primary pathway of your parasympathetic nervous system, in other words, the relaxation response and when you activate your vagus nerve, you send a signal to your brain that says, "It's safe to relax now."

One of the most powerful ways to stimulate your vagus nerve is through your breath, specifically through slow, deep breathing with an emphasis on the exhale. When you exhale slowly and fully, you activate pressure receptors in your lungs and heart that send signals up the vagus nerve to your brain, triggering the relaxation response.

Research using heart rate variability (HRV) as a measure of autonomic nervous system function has shown that slow-paced breathing significantly increases vagal tone, essentially strengthening the relaxation response (we covered this in Chapter 1).

. . .

The Exhale Is Key

Most people don't realize that your heart rate actually changes slightly with each breath. When you inhale, your heart rate speeds up slightly. When you exhale, it slows down. This is called respiratory sinus arrhythmia, and it's a sign of a healthy, flexible nervous system.

When you're stressed or anxious, your breathing becomes shallow and rapid, with short exhales. This keeps your heart rate elevated and maintains sympathetic nervous system activation, the opposite of what you need for sleep. When you deliberately slow your breathing and extend your exhale, you're essentially hacking this system, using your breath to slow your heart rate and activate the relaxation response.

This is why all three techniques in this chapter emphasize the exhale. Whether you're holding your breath between inhale and exhale (4-7-8 technique), breathing in a balanced pattern (box breathing), or simply making your exhale longer than your inhale (natural breathing), the extended exhale is what triggers the relaxation response.

Attention and Distraction

Breathing techniques serve a second crucial function. They give your mind something neutral to focus on, preventing it from spiraling into anxious thoughts. When you're counting breaths or focusing on the sensation of air moving in and out, you're redirecting attention away from worries about tomorrow or regrets about today.

This is a form of attentional control i.e. you're choosing where to place your focus. Racing thoughts thrive when your attention wanders freely. Breathing techniques anchor your attention, breaking the cycle of rumination that keeps you awake.

Research on pre-sleep cognitive arousal, the racing thoughts that prevent sleep, has found that techniques that redirect attention away from worries and toward neutral stimuli significantly reduce the time it takes to fall asleep. Breathing is one of the most effective neutral stimuli because it's always available and naturally rhythmic.

Technique 1: The 4-7-8 Breath (The Classic)

We introduced this technique briefly in Chapter 4. Now let's explore it in depth.

The 4-7-8 breathing technique was popularized by Dr. Andrew Weil, who adapted it from pranayama yoga breathing practices. The pattern is simple: inhale for 4 counts, hold for 7 counts, exhale for 8 counts. The extended exhale and the breath hold create a powerful parasympathetic response.

Research examining the 4-7-8 breathing technique has found that it significantly affects heart rate variability, blood pressure, and markers of stress. A study published in Physiological Reports found that practicing 4-7-8 breathing improved heart rate variability and reduced blood pressure, indicating enhanced parasympathetic nervous system activity. (more simply, improved relaxation).6

Another study examining the effects of 4-7-8 breathing on anxiety in post-surgical patients found that it significantly reduced anxiety levels and improved subjective relaxation. The technique was particularly effective for people experiencing acute stress or anxiety.

The breath hold (the "7" in 4-7-8) serves a specific purpose: it increases carbon dioxide levels slightly in your bloodstream, which triggers a deeper, more complete exhale. This isn't dangerous, you're not holding your breath long enough to cause any harm. You're simply creating a physiological condition that makes the exhale more effective.

How to Practice 4-7-8 Breathing

Step 1: Get into position Sit comfortably in a chair with your back supported, or lie down in bed if you're ready to sleep. Place one hand on your chest and one hand on your belly to help you feel your breath.

Step 2: Complete exhale Before you begin the pattern, exhale completely through your mouth, making a "whoosh" sound. Empty your lungs fully. This is your starting point.

Step 3: The pattern

1. Inhale through your nose for 4 counts (silently count: 1, 2, 3, 4)

- Breathe quietly and smoothly
- Feel your belly expand (diaphragmatic breathing)
- Don't force it and breathe to a comfortable fullness

2. Hold your breath for 7 counts (silently count: 1, 2, 3, 4, 5, 6, 7)

- Keep your throat and chest relaxed
- Don't tense up, this is a gentle hold
- If 7 feels too long initially, start with 4-5 and build up

3. Exhale through your mouth for 8 counts (silently count: 1, 2, 3, 4, 5, 6, 7, 8)

- Make a "whoosh" sound as you exhale
- Empty your lungs completely
- Let your belly fall naturally

Step 4: Repeat This is one cycle. Repeat for 4 cycles total (about 3-4 minutes). As you become more comfortable with the technique, you can extend to 8 cycles (about 6-8 minutes).

The ratio matters more than the speed. If counting to 4-7-8 feels too fast or too slow, adjust the speed of your counting. Some people count "one-one-thousand, two-one-thousand" to slow it down. Find a pace that feels comfortable but still creates a noticeable extended exhale.

This should never feel forced or uncomfortable. If holding for 7 feels like too much, start with a 4-4-6 pattern and gradually work up to 4-7-8 over several days or weeks.

The exhale sound is also optional. The "whoosh" sound is traditional and helps some people fully exhale, but if it feels silly or uncomfortable, you can exhale silently. The important part is the complete exhale.

You might also feel lightheaded at first. This is normal and usually passes after a few practice sessions. If it persists, slow down your breathing or reduce the number of cycles.

When to Use 4-7-8

Best for: High anxiety, racing thoughts, acute stress, difficulty falling asleep initially

Timing: During your wind-down routine (minutes 6-10), or when you get into bed and notice your mind is racing

Not ideal for: If you find breath-holding uncomfortable or if you have respiratory conditions that make breath-holding difficult (in which case, skip to Technique 3)

Technique 2: Box Breathing (The Military Method)

Box breathing, also called square breathing or four-square breathing, is used by Navy SEALs, athletes, and first responders to manage stress in high-pressure situations. The pattern is perfectly balanced: inhale for 4, hold for 4, exhale for 4, hold for 4. This creates a "box" or "square" pattern that's easy to remember and practice.

Box breathing triggers your relaxation response through a combination of slow breathing and the brief breath holds. Research has shown that box breathing reduces stress markers, lowers blood pressure, and improves heart rate variability.

A study examining the effects of box breathing found that it significantly increased parasympathetic nervous system activity and reduced sympathetic nervous system activity, as measured by heart rate variability. Participants reported feeling calmer and more focused after just a few minutes of practice.

The balanced pattern of box breathing makes it particularly effective for people who feel overwhelmed or out of control. The symmetry is psychologically calming, there's no complexity to remember, just four equal parts. This simplicity allows you to focus fully on the breath without cognitive load.

How to Practice Box Breathing

Step 1: Get into position Sit comfortably or lie down. Close your eyes if that feels comfortable, or keep them open with a soft gaze.

Step 2: Visualize a box Some people find it helpful to visualize tracing the sides of a box as they breathe:

- Inhale = trace up the left side
- Hold = trace across the top
- Exhale = trace down the right side
- Hold = trace across the bottom

This visualization is optional but can help anchor your attention.

Step 3: The pattern

1. Exhale completely to empty your lungs (this is your starting point)

2. Inhale through your nose for 4 counts (1, 2, 3, 4)

   - Breathe smoothly and steadily
   - Fill your lungs comfortably

3. Hold your breath for 4 counts (1, 2, 3, 4)

   - Keep your throat and chest relaxed
   - Don't tense up

4. Exhale through your nose or mouth for 4 counts (1, 2, 3, 4)

   - Release the breath smoothly and completely
   - Empty your lungs fully

5. Hold empty for 4 counts (1, 2, 3, 4)

   - Keep your lungs empty but relaxed
   - Don't gasp for the next breath

Step 4: Repeat This is one cycle. Repeat for 5-10 cycles (about 3-6 minutes). You can extend to 15-20 cycles (about 8-10 minutes) as you become more comfortable.

Adjust the count if you need to. If 4 counts feels too short or too long, adjust to 3 or 5. You are only aiming for equal counts for all four parts. A 3-3-3-3 pattern is just as effective as 4-4-4-4 if it feels more comfortable.

Some people find holding their breath with empty lungs uncomfortable. If that's you, use a 4-4-4-0 pattern (inhale-hold-exhale-no hold), or switch to Technique 3.

Also try to breathe through your nose when possible. This is because nasal breathing is generally more calming than mouth breathing, but if you're congested, mouth breathing is fine.

And don't force the breath holds - if you need to breathe before the count is complete, that's okay. Take a natural breath and resume the pattern. This isn't a test of lung capacity - it's a relaxation technique.

When to Use Box Breathing

Best for: General stress reduction, when you need to feel grounded and centered, if 4-7-8 feels too complex

Timing: During your wind-down routine, during the day when you notice stress building, or anytime you need to reset

Not ideal for: If breath-holding feels uncomfortable or triggering (in which case, use Technique 3)

Technique 3: Natural Breathing with Extended Exhale (The Gentle Option)

This is the simplest and gentlest of the three techniques. There's no breath-holding, no counting to specific numbers, and no complex pattern to remember. You simply breathe naturally, with one modification: make your exhale noticeably longer than your inhale.

Research on slow-paced breathing has consistently shown that the key factor in activating the parasympathetic nervous system is the length and completeness of the exhale. You don't need to hold your breath or follow a complex pattern, simply extending your exhale is sufficient to trigger the relaxation response.

A systematic review examining slow breathing (generally defined as 6 breaths per minute or fewer) found that it significantly increased heart rate variability and reduced markers of stress and anxiety. The studies included in the review used various breathing patterns, but the common factor was slow, deep breathing with full exhales.

Another study specifically examining the effects of slow-paced breathing on sleep found that a 30-day intervention of slow breathing practice improved subjective sleep quality and cardiovascular function during sleep. Participants practiced just 10 minutes per day, and the benefits were sustained over time.

This technique is particularly valuable for people who find structured breathing patterns anxiety-inducing. Some people report that counting or holding their breath makes them more anxious, not less. If that's you, this method is ideal.

How to Practice Natural Breathing with Extended Exhale

Step 1: Get into position Sit or lie down comfortably. Place one hand on your belly to help you feel your breath.

Step 2: Observe your natural breath For the first minute or so, just notice your breathing without trying to change it. Notice:

- Where do you feel the breath most? (nose, throat, chest, belly)
- Is it fast or slow?
- Shallow or deep?
- Smooth or jagged?

Don't judge. Just observe. This helps you establish a baseline and brings your attention to your breath.

Step 3: Deepen the breath gradually Begin to breathe a little more deeply, letting your belly expand as you inhale. Don't force it, just invite a slightly fuller breath. Imagine you're filling your lungs from the bottom up, like pouring water into a glass.

Step 4: Extend the exhale Now, begin to make your exhale noticeably longer than your inhale. You don't need to count, try to just feel it. The exhale should be slow, smooth, and complete. Empty your lungs fully, letting your belly fall naturally.

A rough guideline: if your inhale takes about 3-4 seconds, let your exhale take 6-8 seconds. But don't get rigid about the numbers, the goal is a natural rhythm where the exhale is clearly longer.

Step 5: Find your rhythm After a few breaths, you'll settle into a natural rhythm. Your body will find a pace that feels sustainable and comfortable. Stay with this rhythm for 5-10 minutes.

And finally...

This should feel easy. If you're straining or feeling out of breath, you're trying too hard. Slow down, take a few natural breaths, and start again more gently.

Your mind will wander and that's completely normal. When you notice your mind has drifted to thoughts about tomorrow or yesterday, gently bring your attention back to the sensation of breathing. No judgment, no frustration, simply a gentle return.

You can count if it helps. Some people like to count "in-2-3-4, out-2-3-4-5-6-7-8" to help maintain the extended exhale. Others find counting distracting. Do what works for you.

Belly breathing is ideal but not required. Diaphragmatic breathing (where your belly expands on the inhale) is more efficient and calming than chest breathing. But if you have difficulty with belly breathing, chest breathing is fine. Don't add stress by trying to breathe "perfectly."

When to Use Natural Breathing with Extended Exhale

Best for: When other techniques feel too structured or anxiety-inducing, for beginners, for extended practice (10-15 minutes), anytime you need gentle calming.

Timing: During your wind-down routine, during the day for stress management, or in the middle of the night if you wake up anxious.

Ideal for: People with respiratory conditions who find breath-holding uncomfortable, people who get anxious with structured counting, anyone who wants the simplest possible technique.

Choosing Your Technique: A Comparison Guide

You don't need to use all three techniques. Choose one that resonates with you and practice it consistently. Use the table below to help you decide.

Situation	Best Technique	Why
High anxiety, racing thoughts	4-7-8 Breathing	The breath hold and extended exhale create a strong parasympathetic response
Need to feel grounded and centered	Box Breathing	The balanced, symmetrical pattern is psychologically calming
Prefer simplicity, find counting stressful	Natural Extended Exhale	No complex pattern to remember, just gentle awareness
First time trying breathing exercises	Box Breathing or Natural Extended Exhale	Easier to learn than 4-7-8
Respiratory conditions or breath-holding feels uncomfortable	Natural Extended Exhale	No breath-holding required
Want a technique for daytime stress	Box Breathing	Can be done discreetly anywhere
Middle-of-night awakening	Natural Extended Exhale	Gentle enough not to wake you further
Part of wind-down routine	Any of the three	Choose based on personal preference

Common Mistakes and How to Fix Them

Mistake 1: Breathing Too Fast

The problem: You're rushing through the counts, trying to "get it done" rather than allowing the breath to be slow and calming.

The fix: Slow down your counting. Try "one-one-thousand, two-one-thousand" to extend each count. Remember, the goal is relaxation, not speed.

Mistake 2: Forcing the Breath

The problem: You're trying to breathe as deeply as possible, filling your lungs to maximum capacity and emptying them completely with force.

The fix: Breathe to about 80% of your capacity. The breath should feel full but not strained. Think "comfortable fullness" on the inhale and "gentle release" on the exhale.

Mistake 3: Tensing Up During Breath Holds

The problem: You're clenching your throat or chest while holding your breath, creating tension instead of relaxation.

The fix: Keep your throat, chest, and shoulders relaxed during the hold. The hold should feel like a gentle pause, not a struggle. If you can't relax during the hold, shorten it or skip it.

Mistake 4: Getting Frustrated When Your Mind Wanders

The problem: You notice your mind has drifted to other thoughts and you judge yourself or feel like you're "failing" at the technique.

The fix: Mind-wandering is completely normal and expected. It's not a failure, it's an opportunity to practice gently redirecting your attention. Each time you notice and return to your breath, you're strengthening your attentional control. Be patient with yourself.

Mistake 5: Expecting Immediate Results

The problem: You try a breathing technique once and expect to fall asleep instantly. When that doesn't happen, you conclude it doesn't work.

The fix: Breathing techniques become more effective with practice. Your nervous system needs to learn the association between the breathing pattern and relaxation. Give it at least a week of consistent practice before judging effectiveness.

Mistake 6: Only Using It When Desperate

The problem: You only try breathing techniques when you're already extremely anxious and unable to sleep, which is the hardest time to learn a new skill.

The fix: Practice during the day when you're calm. This trains your nervous system to respond to the technique, making it more effective when you really need it at night.

Building Your Practice

Here's a realistic plan for integrating breathing techniques into your life:

Week 1: Daytime Practice

Practice your chosen technique for 5 minutes once per day, ideally in the afternoon or early evening. Don't wait until bedtime, and practice when you're relatively calm so you can learn the pattern without the pressure of needing it to work immediately.

Week 2: Add to Wind-Down Routine

Continue your daytime practice, and add the technique to your wind-down routine (minutes 6-10 from Chapter 4). You're now practicing twice per day.

Week 3: Use as Needed

Continue your wind-down routine practice, and start using the technique whenever you notice stress or anxiety during the day. You're building a conditioned response, your body is learning that this breathing pattern means "time to relax."

Week 4 and Beyond: Maintain and Refine

By now, the technique should feel natural. Continue using it as part of your wind-down routine. You might also find yourself automatically using it in stressful situations, that's a sign it's become integrated into your stress management toolkit.

What to Expect

First few times: The technique might feel awkward or mechanical. You might not notice much effect. That's normal, you're learning a new skill.

After a few days: The pattern becomes more natural. You might notice your body starting to relax during the practice, even if it doesn't immediately make you sleepy.

After 1-2 weeks: You'll likely notice that starting the breathing technique triggers a relaxation response more quickly. Your body is learning the association.

After 3-4 weeks: The technique becomes automatic. You can do it without thinking about the mechanics, and your body responds reliably with relaxation.

How the Pieces Fit

Let's go back to Tom from the beginning of this chapter, lying in bed with a racing mind and tense body. Here's what changed for him.

Tom chose box breathing because he liked the simplicity and symmetry. For the first week, he practiced for 5 minutes every afternoon at his desk. It felt strange at first, but by day 4, he noticed his shoulders dropping and his jaw unclenching during the practice.

In week 2, he added box breathing to his wind-down routine. He would sit on the edge of his bed, dim the lights, and practice 10 cycles of box breathing (about 5 minutes) before getting under the covers. Some nights he felt noticeably calmer afterward. Other nights, not much changed. He kept practicing anyway, remembering the 80/20 principle from Chapter 2, consistency matters more than perfection.

By week 3, Tom noticed something interesting: as soon as he started the breathing pattern, his body began to relax. He didn't have to complete 10 cycles to feel the effect because the first few breaths triggered the response. His body had learned the association.

Now, three months later, box breathing is as automatic as brushing his teeth. It's part of his wind-down routine, and it's also his go-to tool when he notices stress building during the day. He still has nights when sleep is difficult, but he has a tool that reliably helps him shift from "wired" to "ready for rest."

That's why breathing can work - it's simple, it's free, it's always available, and it works with your biology instead of against it.

What You Need to Remember

Your breath is a bridge between conscious control and automatic physiological response. By changing your breathing pattern, you can activate your parasympathetic nervous system and trigger the relaxation response.

The exhale is key. Extended, complete exhales stimulate the vagus nerve and slow your heart rate, signaling to your body that it's safe to relax.

Three evidence-based techniques:

- 4-7-8 Breathing: Inhale 4, hold 7, exhale 8. Best for high anxiety and racing thoughts.
- Box Breathing: Inhale 4, hold 4, exhale 4, hold 4. Best for feeling grounded and centered.
- Natural Extended Exhale: Breathe naturally with exhale longer than inhale. Best for simplicity and gentleness.

Choose one technique and practice consistently. Don't try to master all three at once. Pick the one that feels most comfortable and practice it daily.

Practice during the day first. Learn the technique when you're calm, so it's available when you need it at night.

Be patient. Your nervous system needs 1-2 weeks to learn the association between the breathing pattern and relaxation.

Mind-wandering is normal. Gently redirect your attention back to your breath without judgment.

In the next chapter, we'll explore another powerful relaxation technique: the body scan. While breathing works from the inside out (using internal physiology to calm the mind), body scan works from the outside in (using awareness of physical sensations to release tension and quiet thoughts). Together, these techniques give you multiple pathways to the same destination: a calm body and quiet mind ready for sleep.

Chapter 6

Body Scan for Sleep

Lisa is lying in bed, mentally reviewing her day. She's thinking about the meeting that didn't go well, the text she needs to respond to, the groceries she forgot to buy. Her mind is fully engaged, racing from one thought to the next. Meanwhile, like Tom, her body is sending signals she's completely ignoring. Her jaw is clenched, her shoulders are hunched up near her ears, her hands are balled into fists, and her breathing is shallow. She's so caught up in her thoughts that she has no awareness of the physical tension she's carrying.

This disconnect between mind and body is one of the most common barriers to sleep. Your mind can be thinking about tomorrow while your body is still holding the stress of today. You can't relax what you're not aware of.

That's where body scan meditation comes in. While breathing techniques that Tom used work by using breath to influence your nervous system, body scan works by bringing awareness to physical sensations. You systematically move your attention through different parts of your body, noticing tension and consciously releasing it. It's a practice of reconnecting mind and body, and in doing so, creating the conditions for sleep and, by the end of this chapter, you'll have another powerful tool for your wind-down routine.

THE SCIENCE OF BODY SCAN MEDITATION

Body scan meditation comes from the mindfulness-based stress reduction (MBSR) tradition, developed by Jon Kabat-Zinn in the 1970s. It's been extensively studied for its effects on stress, anxiety, pain, and sleep.

How Body Awareness Helps Sleep

When you're stressed or anxious, your body holds tension in predictable places: jaw, neck, shoulders, back, stomach. This physical tension sends signals to your brain that there's a threat, which keeps your sympathetic nervous system (the stress response) activated. As we learned in Chapter 1, you can't sleep when your sympathetic nervous system is dominant. You need your parasympathetic nervous system (the relaxation response) to take over.

Body scan meditation interrupts this cycle by bringing conscious awareness to tension. Research in neuroscience has shown that simply noticing physical sensations, without trying to change them, begins to reduce the intensity of those sensations. When you add the intention to release tension, the effect is even stronger.

A study examining the effects of body scan meditation on sleep found that participants who practiced body scan regularly reported significant improvements in sleep quality, reduced time to fall asleep, and fewer nighttime awakenings. The researchers noted that this technique was particularly effective for people whose insomnia was related to physical tension and pre-sleep arousal.

Another study specifically examined the addition of this meditation to cognitive behavioral therapy for insomnia (CBT-I) in adolescents.

The results showed that the group using body scan had additional improvements in objective sleep measures beyond standard CBT-I, particularly in reducing wake time after sleep onset.

The Attention Training Effect

Body scan serves a second crucial function by training your attention. When you practice moving your awareness systematically through your body, you're strengthening your ability to direct your attention intentionally. This is the opposite of rumination, where your attention is hijacked by anxious thoughts.

Research on mindfulness meditation, which includes body scan as a core practice, has found that regular practice increases activity in brain regions associated with attention control and decreases activity in the "default mode network," the brain network responsible for mind-wandering and rumination. For people with insomnia, who often struggle with racing thoughts at bedtime, this attention training is particularly valuable.

Letting Go

Body scan doesn't work by forcing your body to relax but by noticing what's already there, without judgment or effort to change it. This sits perfectly with the anti-perfectionism principle from Chapter 2. You're not trying to achieve perfect relaxation. You're simply observing your body with curiosity and kindness.

This non-striving attitude often produces more relaxation than trying hard to relax. When you stop fighting against tension and simply acknowledge it, the tension often releases on its own. This is similar to the paradoxical intention technique we discussed in Chapter 2.

The Basic 10-Minute Scan

Here's a complete sequence that takes about 10 minutes. You can practice this during your wind-down routine (minutes 6-10 from Chapter 4), or when you're already in bed and ready to sleep.

Preparation

Position: Lie down on your back in bed, or sit in a comfortable chair if lying down isn't possible. If you're in bed, you can be under the covers or on top of them, whatever feels comfortable.

Arms and legs: Let your arms rest at your sides, palms facing up if that's comfortable. Let your legs be slightly apart, feet falling naturally to the sides.

Eyes: You can keep your eyes closed, or open with a soft gaze toward the ceiling. Most people find closed eyes easier, but do what works for you.

Breath: Breathe naturally. You don't need to control your breath during body scan (though you can combine it with the extended exhale from Chapter 5 if you like).

The Sequence

I'll give you the full script here. When you practice, you can read this slowly to yourself, have someone read it to you, or simply remember the general sequence and move through it at your own pace.

Beginning (1 minute)

"I'm lying here, taking a few moments to arrive in this practice. I notice the weight of my body against the bed (or chair). I notice the rhythm of my breathing, without trying to change it. I'm here, in this moment, ready to bring kind attention to my body."

Take three slow, full breaths. Notice the sensation of breathing.

Feet (1 minute)

"I bring my attention to my feet. Both feet. I notice any sensations: warmth or coolness, tingling, pressure where they touch the bed or floor, or perhaps no particular sensation at all. Whatever I notice is fine. I'm not trying to feel anything specific, just observing what's here."

"If I notice tension in my feet, I can imagine breathing into that area, and as I exhale, letting the tension soften and release. If there's no tension, that's fine too."

Lower legs (1 minute)

"I move my attention up to my lower legs. My ankles, shins, calves. I notice the sensations here. Perhaps the weight of my legs against the bed. Perhaps tingling or warmth. Perhaps nothing in particular. All of this is okay."

"I can imagine my lower legs becoming heavy and relaxed, sinking into the bed with each exhale."

Upper legs (1 minute)

"I bring attention to my upper legs. My knees, thighs. I notice any sensations. I notice the contact between my legs and the bed beneath me. If there's tension here, I can invite it to soften. If there's no tension, I simply observe what's present."

Hips and pelvis (30 seconds)

"I move my awareness to my hips and pelvis. This is where many people hold tension without realizing it. I notice any tightness or gripping here. I can imagine this area softening, releasing, letting go with each exhale."

Abdomen and lower back (1 minute)

"I bring attention to my abdomen and lower back. I notice my belly rising and falling with each breath. I notice any sensations in my lower back, perhaps where it contacts the bed. If there's tension here, I acknowledge it without judgment. I can imagine breathing into this area, and as I exhale, letting any tightness go."

Chest and upper back (1 minute)

"I move my awareness to my chest and upper back. I notice my breath moving in this area. I notice any sensations: openness or tightness, warmth or coolness. If my chest feels tight or constricted, I can imagine it expanding slightly with each inhale, softening with each exhale."

Hands and arms (1 minute)

"I bring attention to my hands. Both hands. I notice my fingers, palms, the backs of my hands. Perhaps there's tingling or warmth. Perhaps my hands feel heavy. I'm simply observing."

"I move my awareness up through my forearms, elbows, upper arms. I notice any sensations here. I can imagine my arms becoming heavy and relaxed, releasing any holding or tension."

Shoulders and neck (1 minute)

"I bring attention to my shoulders and neck. This is where many of us carry the weight of our day. I notice if my shoulders are hunched or tense. I notice any tightness in my neck. I'm not judging this tension, just acknowledging it."

"I can imagine my shoulders dropping down away from my ears, releasing and softening. I can imagine my neck lengthening, any tightness melting away."

Face and head (1 minute)

"I bring attention to my face. My jaw (am I clenching?), my cheeks, my eyes, my forehead. I notice any tension here. So many of us hold tension in our faces without realizing it."

"I can imagine my jaw releasing, my teeth slightly apart. My eyes softening in their sockets. My forehead smooth and relaxed. My whole face slowly relaxing, like ice melting."

"I notice my whole head, resting heavily on the pillow."

Whole body (1 minute)

"Now I expand my awareness to include my whole body at once. I notice my body as a complete whole, lying here, breathing. I notice the overall sense of my body: perhaps heavy, perhaps relaxed, perhaps still holding some tension. Whatever is here is okay."

"I take three more slow, full breaths, noticing my whole body with each breath."

Ending

"If I'm ready to sleep, I can simply let my awareness drift, allowing sleep to come naturally. If I'm not quite ready, I can remain here, breathing quietly, or I can gently open my eyes and continue my wind-down routine."

Important Notes

There's no "right" sensation. Some people feel tingling, warmth, heaviness, or coolness during body scan. Others feel very little. Both are completely normal. You're not trying to manufacture specific sensations. You're simply noticing what's already there.

If you're doing this in bed at night, you might fall asleep halfway through. That's not a failure. That's success. The body scan did its job. Don't worry about completing the whole sequence.

Your mind will wander and this is absolutely normal and expected. You might start scanning your feet and suddenly realize you're thinking about tomorrow's meeting. That's okay. Simply notice that your mind wandered, and gently bring your attention back to wherever you left off in the body scan. Each time you notice and return, you're strengthening your attention control.

Some people feel more restless when they first start body scan, not less. This is because you're becoming aware of sensations and tension you were previously ignoring. This typically passes after a few practice sessions as your body learns to release tension rather than just notice it.

The only way to "fail" at this is to judge yourself harshly for not doing it perfectly. Remember Chapter 2: this is not a performance. It's a practice of gentle awareness and it can't be done 'wrong'.

The Quick 5-Minute Scan

Some nights you don't have 10 minutes, or you're already very tired and want a shorter practice. Here's an abbreviated version that hits the key areas:

Minute 1: Feet and legs (both lower and upper together)

Minute 2: Hips, abdomen, and lower back

Minute 3: Chest, upper back, arms and hands

Minute 4: Shoulders, neck, and face

Minute 5: Whole body awareness and three full breaths

The principle is the same. Bring awareness to each area, notice sensations, invite release of tension. You're just moving through the body more quickly.

The Extended 15-Minute Scan

On nights when you're particularly tense or anxious, or when you have more time, you can extend the body scan to 15 minutes. This allows you to spend more time in each area, really noticing subtle sensations and giving tension more time to release.

The sequence is the same as the 10-minute version, but you spend about 2 minutes in each major area (feet and legs, torso, arms, shoulders and neck, face and head) and 3 minutes on whole-body awareness at the end.

You can also add more detail. For example, in the feet section, you might notice each toe individually. In the hands section, you might notice each finger. The slower pace allows for deeper relaxation.

SUBTLE EXPERIMENTATION

Once you're comfortable with the basic exercise, you can experiment with varying what you are doing.

Visualization

As you move through each body part, imagine a warm, golden light moving through that area, melting away tension. Or imagine each area becoming heavy and sinking into the bed. Or imagine tension draining out of each body part like water flowing downward and out through your feet.

Visualization can improve the relaxation effect for some people. Experiment to see if it helps you, but don't feel you must use it. The basic body scan is effective on its own.

Progressive Muscle Relaxation

You can combine body scan with the progressive muscle relaxation technique that we'll cover in the next chapter. As you bring awareness to each body part, gently tense the muscles in that area for 3-5 seconds, then release and notice the contrast between tension and relaxation.

This combination is particularly effective if you have a lot of physical tension or if you find it hard to notice subtle sensations without the contrast of tension and release.

Extended Exhale Breathing

Combine the session with the natural extended exhale breathing from Chapter 5. As you bring awareness to each body part, imagine breathing into that area on the inhale, and releasing tension from that area on the exhale.

This adds the relaxation-inducing breath work to the awareness practice of body scan, creating a powerful combined effect.

Troubleshooting Common Challenges

Challenge 1: "I can't feel anything"

What's happening: Some people, especially when they first start, report feeling very little sensation during body scan. This is often because we're not accustomed to paying attention to subtle body sensations.

What to do: That's okay. You don't need to feel strong sensations for body scan to work. Simply bring your attention to each area, even if you don't notice much. Over time, your awareness will become more refined. You can also try the variation with progressive muscle relaxation, which creates more obvious sensations.

Challenge 2: "My mind wanders constantly"

What's happening: This is completely normal, especially for people with anxiety or insomnia. Your brain is used to racing from thought to thought.

What to do: Each time you notice your mind has wandered, silently say to yourself "thinking" or "wandering," then gently return to the body scan. Don't judge yourself. The practice is not about maintaining perfect focus. The practice is about noticing when you've lost focus and returning, over and over. Each return strengthens your attention control.

Challenge 3: "I feel more anxious, not less"

What's happening: Sometimes when you first start noticing your body, you become aware of how much tension you're carrying, which can feel overwhelming. Or you might feel anxious about "doing it right."

What to do: Remember that awareness is the first step to release. It's okay to notice tension. You're not trying to force it away. Simply acknowledge it: "There's tension in my shoulders. That's okay." If the anxiety persists, you might find breathing techniques (Chapter 5) more helpful initially. Return to body scan after you've practiced breathing for a week or two.

Challenge 4: "I fall asleep too quickly"

What's happening: You're falling asleep before you finish, and you feel like you're "not doing it right."

What to do: This is not a problem. This is the goal. If you're doing this in bed at night and you fall asleep during it, the technique is working. You don't need to complete the entire sequence. The purpose is to facilitate sleep, not to stay awake through the whole practice.

Challenge 5: "I feel restless and want to move"

What's happening: Lying still and bringing awareness to your body can sometimes make you feel restless, especially if you're used to constant movement or distraction.

What to do: It's okay to adjust your position if you need to. It isn't about forcing yourself to stay perfectly still. If you need to scratch an itch or shift your weight, do so mindfully and then return to the practice. The restlessness often decreases after a few sessions as your body learns to settle.

Challenge 6: "I don't have time to practice during the day"

What's happening: You're only doing body scan at night when you're trying to sleep, which means you're learning the technique under pressure.

What to do: If possible, practice it once during the day when you're not trying to sleep. This could be during a lunch break, in the afternoon, or early evening. Practicing when you're not desperate for sleep helps you learn the technique more easily. But if you truly can't find daytime time, nighttime practice is still valuable.

Building Your Practice

Here's a realistic way to integrate this work into your life:

Week 1: Learn the Sequence

Practice the 10-minute scan once a day, ideally in the afternoon or early evening. Remember, don't worry about doing it perfectly. Just familiarize yourself with the general sequence: feet, legs, torso, arms, shoulders and neck, face, whole body.

You can read the script slowly, or use a guided recording if that helps (many free body scan recordings are available online).

Week 2: Add to Wind-Down Routine

Continue your daytime practice if possible, and add body scan to your wind-down routine. You can use it as your relaxation technique in minutes 6-10 from Chapter 4.

Some nights you might prefer this exercise. Other nights you might prefer breathing (Chapter 5). That's fine. You're building a toolkit, not committing to one technique forever.

Week 3: Experiment with Variations

Try the quick 5-minute version on busy nights. Try the extended 15-minute version when you're particularly tense. Try adding visualization or combining with breathing. Find what works best for you.

Week 4 and Beyond: Maintain and Refine

By now, body scan should feel more natural. You might not need to follow the script anymore. You might have developed your own rhythm and pace. Continue using it as part of your wind-down routine, or whenever you notice physical tension during the day.

COMBINING BODY SCAN WITH OTHER TECHNIQUES

Body scan works beautifully in combination with other techniques from this book:

After breathing: Start with 3-4 cycles of 4-7-8 breathing or box breathing (Chapter 5) to calm your nervous system, then move into body scan. This combination is particularly effective for high anxiety.

With worry dump: Do your worry dump (Chapter 2) first to clear mental clutter, then do body scan to release physical tension. This addresses both cognitive and physical arousal.

As part of wind-down ritual: Dim lights and put away screens (minutes 1-2), do gentle stretching (minutes 3-5), then body scan (minutes 6-10). This creates a complete transition from activity to rest.

For middle-of-night awakenings: If you wake up at 3 AM and can't fall back asleep, body scan can help you relax back into sleep. We'll talk more about this in a later chapter.

What to Expect Over Time

First few times: It might feel awkward or mechanical. You might not notice much effect. Your mind will wander frequently. This is all normal.

After one week: The sequence becomes more familiar. You might start noticing tension you weren't aware of before. Your mind still wanders, but you're getting better at noticing and returning.

After two weeks: You might start feeling relaxation during the practice, even if you don't fall asleep immediately. Your body is beginning to learn the association between body scan and relaxation.

After three to four weeks: Body scan work becomes more automatic. You might not need to follow a script. Your body responds more quickly to the practice. You might fall asleep before finishing the sequence, which is a good sign.

Long term: The practice becomes a reliable tool for releasing physical tension and preparing for sleep. You might also find yourself using body awareness throughout the day, noticing tension as it arises and releasing it before it accumulates.

Back to Lisa

Returning to Lisa who was lying in bed with her mind racing and her body tense as we started this chapter.

Lisa began with the 10-minute body scan, practicing in the late afternoon while lying on her living room floor. The first few times, she felt restless and her mind wandered constantly. She kept thinking she was "doing it wrong." But she remembered the anti-perfectionism principle from Chapter 2 and kept practicing anyway.

By the end of week one, she noticed that during the body scan, she became aware of how much tension she was holding in her jaw and shoulders. She had been clenching her jaw all day without realizing it. This awareness alone helped her start releasing tension throughout the day, not just during the practice.

In week two, she added it to her bedtime routine. Some nights she combined it with breathing exercises. Other nights she did it alone. She noticed that on nights when she did body scan, she fell asleep more quickly and woke up less during the night.

By week four, the technique had become automatic. She no longer needed to follow a script. She would lie in bed, bring awareness to her feet, and often fall asleep before reaching her shoulders. Her body had learned that body scan meant "time to sleep."

These days, Lisa will still experience the occasional restless night, but she notices her tension earlier in the day and has a way to cope before it builds up. She's also developed what she calls "body check-ins," a few minutes throughout the day when she checks to see where she's holding tension and consciously releases it. Her chronic jaw pain has decreased, and her sleep has improved.

That's why body awareness is so good. It reconnects mind and body, releases built-up tension, and creates the physical conditions for sleep.

A Few Things to Hold Onto

Body scan meditation works by bringing conscious awareness to physical sensations throughout your body. You systematically move attention from feet to head, noticing tension and inviting release.

The basic sequence takes 10 minutes: Feet, legs, hips and pelvis, abdomen and back, chest and upper back, arms and hands, shoulders and neck, face and head, whole body.

You can't do it wrong. The only mistake is judging yourself harshly for not doing it perfectly. Mind-wandering is normal. Falling asleep before finishing is actually success.

Three variations: Quick 5-minute version for busy nights, extended 15-minute version for high tension, and enhancements like visualization or combining with breathing.

Practice during the day first if possible. Learning the technique when you're not desperate for sleep makes it more effective when you need it at night.

The exercise works differently than breathing. Breathing influences your nervous system directly through physiology. Body scan works through awareness and attention. Both are valuable tools.

Falling asleep during this process is the goal, not a failure. If you're doing this in bed at night and you fall asleep halfway through, the technique is working.

Give it two to three weeks. Your body needs time to learn the association between body scan and relaxation.

In the next chapter, we'll explore progressive muscle relaxation (PMR), a technique that combines elements of both breathing and body scan. PMR uses active tensing and releasing of muscles to create deep physical relaxation. While body scan is passive awareness, PMR is active release. Together, these techniques give you multiple ways to the same destination: a relaxed body ready for sleep.

Chapter 7

Progressive Muscle Relaxation (PMR)

Many people know they need to wind down but simply don't know how to relax in the first place, and it doesn't matter how often you tell yourself to "just relax," because nothing happens.

And many of us have been tense for so long that we've forgotten what relaxation actually feels like. We've lost the ability to consciously release muscle tension. Our bodies are stuck in a chronic state of low-level contraction, maintaining the stress response even when there's no immediate threat.

Progressive muscle relaxation (PMR) solves this problem by teaching your body what relaxation feels like through contrast. You deliberately tense a muscle group for a few seconds, then release it completely. The release creates a wave of relaxation that's much more noticeable than if you had simply tried to relax without tensing first. Over time, your body relearns how to release tension on command.

In this chapter, you'll learn a complete 8 to 10 minute PMR sequence that you can use as part of your wind-down routine. You'll learn exactly how much tension to use, which muscle groups to target, and how to avoid common mistakes. By the end, you'll have another powerful tool for releasing physical tension and preparing your body for sleep.

The Science of Progressive Muscle Relaxation

PMR was developed in the 1920s by American physician Edmund Jacobson, who noticed that muscle tension was a key component of anxiety and stress. He theorized that if you could eliminate muscle tension, you could reduce anxiety and promote relaxation. His original technique involved tensing and relaxing over 200 different muscle groups, which took hours to complete. Modern PMR uses a condensed version targeting 7 to 14 major muscle groups, taking just 10 to 20 minutes.

How Tensing Leads to Relaxation

This seems counterintuitive because how can creating tension lead to relaxation? The answer lies in several mechanisms.

First, the contrast effect. When you tense a muscle and then release it, the relaxation you experience is much more noticeable than if you had simply tried to relax without tensing first. This helps you recognize what relaxation actually feels like in your body, training your awareness.

Second, muscle fatigue. When you tense a muscle for several seconds, you temporarily fatigue it slightly. When you release, the muscle naturally relaxes more completely than it was before you tensed it. You're essentially "resetting" the muscle to a lower baseline tension.

Third, attention and awareness. PMR requires you to focus on specific body parts, which redirects your attention away from anxious thoughts. Like body scan (Chapter 6), it's a form of attentional control that interrupts rumination.

Fourth, the physiological relaxation response. Research has shown that PMR activates the parasympathetic nervous system, the same "rest and digest" system we discussed at the start of the book. Studies measuring heart rate variability, blood pressure, and cortisol levels have found that PMR produces measurable physiological relaxation.

The Research Evidence

PMR is one of the most well-researched relaxation techniques, with decades of studies supporting its effectiveness for anxiety, stress, and sleep problems.

A comprehensive review examining the effectiveness of PMR, deep breathing, and guided imagery found that all three techniques increased relaxation, but PMR had particularly strong effects on reducing physical tension and physiological arousal.

And a study specifically examining PMR's effects on sleep found that it increased slow-wave sleep (the deepest, most restorative stage) during the first sleep cycle. Participants who practiced PMR before bed spent more time in deep sleep and reported feeling more rested in the morning.

Multiple studies with various populations (cancer patients, people with chronic pain, individuals with anxiety disorders, older adults with insomnia) have found that regular PMR practice improves sleep quality, reduces time to fall asleep, and decreases nighttime awakenings. And a meta-analysis examining PMR for anxiety found it had a large overall effect size, meaning the benefits were substantial and consistent across studies.

PMR is also a core component of cognitive behavioral therapy for insomnia (CBT-I), the gold-standard treatment for chronic insomnia. Its inclusion in CBT-I protocols is based on strong evidence of effectiveness.

The Basic 8 to 10 Minute PMR Sequence

Here's a complete PMR sequence targeting seven major muscle groups. This takes about 8 to 10 minutes, making it perfect for the relaxation portion of your wind-down routine (minutes 6 to 10 from Chapter 4).

Preparation

Position: Sit in a comfortable chair with your feet flat on the floor and your arms resting on the armrests or in your lap. You can also lie down in bed, though sitting is often better for learning the technique because it's easier to tense muscles effectively.

Clothing: Wear comfortable, loose clothing. Remove glasses, contact lenses if possible, and anything restrictive.

Environment: Dim the lights. You want to be able to focus on your body without visual distractions.

Breathing: Breathe naturally throughout. Don't hold your breath while tensing muscles.

The Tension-Release Pattern

For each muscle group, you'll follow this pattern:

1. Take a breath in
2. Tense the muscle group for 5 to 7 seconds (not so hard it hurts, but enough to feel clear tension)
3. Release suddenly and completely while exhaling
4. Notice the sensation of relaxation for 15 to 20 seconds
5. Move to the next muscle group

The release should be sudden, not gradual. You're letting go all at once, like dropping a heavy weight. This creates the strongest contrast between tension and relaxation.

The Seven Muscle Groups

1. Hands and Forearms (1 minute)

Tense: Make tight fists with both hands. Squeeze as if you're trying to squeeze water out of a sponge. Feel the tension in your hands, knuckles, and forearms.

Hold for 5 to 7 seconds.

Release: Open your hands suddenly, letting your fingers spread apart. Let your hands rest heavily in your lap or on the armrests.

Notice: Feel the wave of relaxation flowing through your hands and forearms. Notice the difference between tension and relaxation. Your hands might feel warm, heavy, or tingly. Whatever you notice is fine.

Wait 15 to 20 seconds, breathing naturally.

2. Upper Arms (1 minute)

Tense: Bend your arms at the elbows and tense your biceps, as if you're showing off your muscles. You can also press your elbows against your sides to engage your triceps. Feel the tension in your upper arms.

Hold for 5 to 7 seconds.

Release: Let your arms drop suddenly, returning to rest in your lap or on the armrests. Let them become heavy and loose.

Notice: Feel the relaxation spreading through your upper arms. Notice the heaviness, the warmth, the sense of letting go.

Wait 15 to 20 seconds.

3. Shoulders and Neck (1.5 minutes)

Tense: Raise your shoulders up toward your ears, as if you're shrugging. At the same time, press your head back slightly (if sitting) or into the pillow (if lying down). Feel the tension across your shoulders and the back of your neck.

Hold for 5 to 7 seconds.

Release: Let your shoulders drop suddenly, falling down and back. Let your head return to a neutral position. Feel your neck lengthen.

Notice: This is where many people hold chronic tension. Really notice the difference between the tension you just created and the relaxation you're experiencing now. Your shoulders might drop lower than they've been all day.

Wait 15 to 20 seconds.

4. Face (1.5 minutes)

Tense: Squeeze your eyes shut tightly. At the same time, wrinkle your nose and raise your cheeks, as if you're squinting in bright sunlight. Clench your jaw, pressing your teeth together. Feel tension across your entire face.

Hold for 5 to 7 seconds.

Release: Let everything go at once. Let your jaw drop slightly, your teeth separating. Let your eyes soften in their sockets. Let your forehead smooth out. Let your whole face become soft and relaxed.

Notice: Many people don't realize how much tension they carry in their faces. Notice how different your face feels when it's truly relaxed. Your jaw might feel loose, your eyes soft, your forehead smooth.

Wait 15 to 20 seconds.

5. Chest and Upper Back (1 minute)

Tense: Take a deep breath in and hold it. At the same time, pull your shoulder blades together behind you, as if you're trying to make them touch. Feel the tension across your chest and between your shoulder blades.

Hold for 5 to 7 seconds.

Release: Exhale completely and let your shoulder blades separate, returning to their natural position. Let your chest soften and relax.

Notice: Feel the relaxation spreading across your chest and upper back. Notice your breathing becoming easier and more natural.

Wait 15 to 20 seconds.

6. Abdomen and Lower Back (1 minute)

Tense: Tighten your stomach muscles, as if you're bracing for a punch or pulling your belly button toward your spine. At the same time, arch your lower back slightly (if sitting) or press it into the chair or bed.

Hold for 5 to 7 seconds.

Release: Let your stomach soften completely. Let your lower back return to its natural curve. Let your whole torso become soft and relaxed.

Notice: Feel the relaxation in your abdomen and lower back. Notice your breathing moving more freely in your belly.

Wait 15 to 20 seconds.

7. Legs and Feet (1.5 minutes)

Tense: Straighten your legs and point your toes away from you (like a ballet dancer). At the same time, tense your thigh muscles. Feel the tension through your entire legs, from hips to toes.

Hold for 5 to 7 seconds.

Release: Let your legs relax completely, bending slightly at the knees if sitting. Let your feet rest naturally on the floor or bed.

Notice: Feel the wave of relaxation flowing down through your thighs, calves, and feet. Your legs might feel heavy, as if they're sinking into the chair or bed.

Wait 15 to 20 seconds.

Whole Body Integration (1 minute)

After completing all seven muscle groups, take a moment to notice your whole body at once. Scan through mentally: hands and arms, shoulders and neck, face, chest and back, abdomen, legs and feet. Notice the overall sense of relaxation.

Take three slow, full breaths, noticing your whole body becoming even more relaxed with each exhale.

If you're ready to sleep, you can simply let your awareness drift. If you're not quite ready, you can remain here for another minute or two, or continue with another part of your wind-down routine.

IMPORTANT GUIDELINES

How Much Tension?

This is the most common question about PMR. The tension should be noticeable and clear, but not painful. On a scale of 1 to 10, where 10 is maximum possible tension, aim for about 6 or 7. You want to feel the muscle working, but you shouldn't be straining or causing discomfort.

If you have any injuries, chronic pain, or physical limitations, reduce the tension level or skip that muscle group entirely. PMR should never hurt.

Don't Hold Your Breath

It's natural to hold your breath when tensing muscles, but try to avoid this. Continue breathing naturally throughout the tension phase. Holding your breath activates the stress response, which is the opposite of what you want.

If you find it difficult to breathe while tensing, you're probably tensing too hard. Reduce the tension level.

The Release Is Key

The moment of release is the most important part of PMR. Let go suddenly and completely, all at once. Don't gradually ease out of the tension. The sudden release creates the strongest relaxation response.

Think of it like dropping a heavy bag you've been carrying. You don't slowly lower it to the ground; you just let it drop.

Focus on the Contrast

During the 15 to 20 seconds after releasing, really pay attention to how the relaxation feels. Notice the difference between the tension you just created and the relaxation you're experiencing now. This trains your body awareness and helps you recognize tension in daily life.

One Side at a Time or Both?

The sequence I've given you works both sides of the body simultaneously (both hands, both arms, etc.). This is faster and works well for most people. However, if you prefer, you can work one side at a time (right hand, then left hand, etc.). This takes longer (about 15 to 20 minutes) but allows for more detailed attention.

Variations and Modifications

The Quick 5-Minute Version

If you're short on time, you can condense PMR to four muscle groups:

1. Hands and arms (both upper and lower together): Make fists and tense biceps simultaneously
2. Face and neck: Scrunch face and raise shoulders together
3. Chest, back, and abdomen: Tense all torso muscles together
4. Legs and feet: Tense entire legs together

Use the same tension-release pattern, but move through the body more quickly.

The Extended 15-Minute Version

For deeper relaxation, you can extend PMR by:

- Working one side of the body at a time (right hand, left hand, right arm, left arm, etc.)
- Repeating each muscle group twice before moving on
- Extending the relaxation phase to 30 seconds instead of 15 to 20

PMR with Visualization

As you release each muscle group, imagine tension draining out of that area like water flowing downward. Or imagine warm, golden light filling the relaxed area. Visualization can enhance the relaxation effect for some people.

PMR Combined with Breathing

You can combine PMR with the extended exhale breathing from Chapter 5. Tense on the inhale, hold briefly, then release on a long, slow exhale. This combines the physical release of PMR with the parasympathetic activation of breathing.

PMR for Specific Problem Areas

If you know you carry tension in particular areas (like shoulders or jaw), you can do extra repetitions of those muscle groups. For example, if your shoulders are chronically tense, you might do the shoulder sequence three times instead of once.

Troubleshooting Common Challenges

Challenge 1: "I get cramps when I tense my muscles"

What's happening: You're tensing too hard, or you're dehydrated, or you're tensing in a way that's prone to cramping (like pointing your toes too forcefully).

What to do: Reduce the tension level significantly. For feet and legs, try flexing your toes toward you instead of pointing them away, which is less likely to cause cramps. Make sure you're well-hydrated. If cramping persists, skip that muscle group.

Challenge 2: "I can't tell if I'm actually relaxed"

What's happening: You've been tense for so long that you've lost awareness of what relaxation feels like.

What to do: This is exactly why PMR is valuable for you. The contrast between tension and release will help you relearn what relaxation feels like. Keep practicing. Your awareness will improve over time. You might also try the extended version with longer relaxation phases, giving yourself more time to notice the sensations.

Challenge 3: "I feel more tense after PMR, not less"

What's happening: Sometimes when you first start PMR, you become more aware of how much tension you're carrying, which can feel uncomfortable. Or you might be trying too hard to "do it right," which creates performance anxiety.

What to do: Remember the anti-perfectionism principle from Chapter 2. You can't do PMR wrong. If it's making you more anxious, try body scan (Chapter 6) or breathing (Chapter 5) instead for a week, then return to PMR. Some people find PMR too activating initially and prefer more passive techniques.

Challenge 4: "I fall asleep before finishing"

What's happening: PMR is working. You're relaxing so deeply that you're falling asleep.

What to do: If you're doing PMR in bed at night, falling asleep before finishing is success, not failure. If you're doing it earlier in your wind-down routine and you don't want to fall asleep yet, practice sitting up rather than lying down, or do it earlier in the evening.

Challenge 5: "My mind wanders during the relaxation phases"

What's happening: This is completely normal. Your mind is used to racing from thought to thought.

What to do: Each time you notice your mind has wandered, gently bring your attention back to the physical sensations in the muscle group you're working on. The practice is not about maintaining perfect focus. The practice is about noticing when you've lost focus and returning. This is the same principle as in body scan (Chapter 6).

Challenge 6: "I have an injury or chronic pain in one area"

What's happening: Tensing an injured or painful area could make it worse.

What to do: Simply skip that muscle group. You can still do PMR with the remaining muscle groups. Or you can do a very gentle version of the tension (maybe 2 or 3 out of 10 instead of 6 or 7) and see if that's tolerable. Never push through pain.

Building Your PMR Practice

Here's a realistic plan to integrating PMR into your life:

Week 1: Learn the Sequence

Practice the full 8 to 10 minute sequence once per day, ideally in the late afternoon or early evening. Sit in a comfortable chair. Follow the script closely until you've memorized the sequence of muscle groups.

Don't worry about doing it perfectly. Just familiarize yourself with the pattern: tense, hold, release, notice.

Week 2: Add to Wind-Down Routine

Continue your daytime practice if possible, and add PMR to your wind-down routine as your relaxation technique (minutes 6 to 10 from Chapter 4).

You now have three relaxation techniques to choose from: breathing (Chapter 5), body scan (Chapter 6), and PMR. Some nights you might prefer one, other nights another. That's fine. You're building a toolkit.

Week 3: Experiment and Refine

Try the quick 5-minute version on busy nights. Try the extended 15-minute version when you're particularly tense. Try combining PMR with breathing or visualization. Find what works best for you.

Pay attention to which muscle groups give you the most relief. You might find that shoulders and neck are your key areas, and you can do extra repetitions there.

Week 4 and Beyond: Maintain and Use as Needed

By now, PMR should feel more natural. You might not need to follow the script anymore. Continue using it as part of your wind-down routine, or whenever you notice physical tension during the day.

Some people use PMR every night. Others use it a few times per week and alternate with other techniques. Both ways are fine.

Comparing the Three Relaxation Techniques

You've now learned three different relaxation techniques. Here's how they compare:

Technique	How It Works	Best For	Time
Breathing (Chapter 5)	Uses breath to activate parasympathetic nervous system	High anxiety, racing thoughts, anytime/anywhere	3 to 10 minutes
Body Scan (Chapter 6)	Uses awareness to release tension	Uses awareness to release tension Reconnecting mind and body, passive relaxation	5 to 15 minutes
PPMR (Chapter 7)	Uses tension-release contrast to teach relaxation	Physical tension, learning what relaxation feels like	5 to 15 minutes

When to use breathing: When you need quick relief, when you're in public and can't tense muscles obviously, when you prefer a subtle technique.

When to use body scan: When you want passive relaxation, when you're already in bed, when you prefer gentle awareness over active tensing.

When to use PMR: When you're carrying a lot of physical tension, when you need the contrast to recognize relaxation, when you prefer an active technique.

Can you combine them?: Absolutely. You might start with breathing to calm your nervous system, then do PMR to release physical tension, then finish with body scan for gentle awareness. Or you might combine PMR with extended exhale breathing. Experiment to find what works for you.

PMR Beyond Bedtime

While this book focuses on sleep, PMR is valuable throughout the day. Once you've learned the technique, you can use it:

During work breaks: A quick 5-minute PMR session can release accumulated tension and improve focus.

Before stressful events: PMR before a presentation, difficult conversation, or medical appointment can reduce anticipatory anxiety.

For pain management: Research has shown PMR can reduce perception of chronic pain by releasing muscle tension that exacerbates pain.

For general stress management: Regular PMR practice (even just 10 minutes per day) reduces overall stress levels and improves resilience.

Many people find that as they practice PMR regularly, they develop the ability to release muscle tension on command without needing to tense first. You might notice tension building in your shoulders during the day and be able to consciously release it. This is a sign that your body has relearned how to relax.

Over the Coming Weeks

First few times: PMR might feel mechanical or awkward. You might not notice dramatic relaxation immediately. You're learning a new skill, and that takes time.

After one week: The sequence becomes more familiar. You start to notice the contrast between tension and relaxation more clearly. You might start recognizing tension in your body during the day.

After two weeks: You begin to feel genuine relaxation during and after PMR. Your body is learning the association between the practice and the relaxation response.

After three to four weeks: PMR becomes more automatic. You might not need to follow a script. You might develop your own variations based on where you carry tension. You might start using mini-PMR sessions throughout the day.

Long term: PMR becomes a reliable tool for releasing physical tension and preparing for sleep. You might also find that your baseline tension level decreases. You're no longer chronically tense because you've taught your body how to release tension regularly.

WHAT MATTERS MOST

Progressive muscle relaxation (PMR) works by deliberately tensing muscles, then releasing them suddenly and completely. The contrast teaches your body what relaxation feels like.

The basic sequence targets seven muscle groups: Hands and forearms, upper arms, shoulders and neck, face, chest and upper back, abdomen and lower back, legs and feet. The full sequence takes 8 to 10 minutes.

The pattern for each muscle group: Tense for 5 to 7 seconds, release suddenly while exhaling, notice the relaxation for 15 to 20 seconds.

Tension should be clear but not painful. Aim for about 6 or 7 out of 10. Never push through pain or discomfort.

The release is the most important part. Let go suddenly and completely, all at once. This creates the strongest relaxation response.

Three variations: Quick 5-minute version for busy nights, extended 15-minute version for deep relaxation, and combinations with breathing or visualization.

PMR is especially effective for physical tension. If your sleep problems are related to carrying tension in your body, PMR is an excellent choice.

You now have three relaxation techniques (breathing, body scan, PMR). Choose based on your needs on any given night, or combine them.

Practice during the day first if possible. Learning PMR when you're not desperate for sleep makes it more effective when you need it at night.

Give it two to three weeks. Your body needs time to relearn what relaxation feels like.

In the next chapter, we'll move from physical relaxation techniques to cognitive techniques for managing racing thoughts. While breathing, body scan, and PMR work primarily with your body, the cognitive techniques in Chapter 8 work directly with your thoughts. Together, these give you comprehensive tools for addressing both the physical and the mental barriers to sleep.

Chapter 8

Cognitive Techniques for Racing Thoughts

You may find yourself lying in bed, and after reading the last chapter, your body is relaxed from the PMR sequence you have just completed. Your muscles are loose, your breathing is slow and steady, but your mind is anything but quiet. You might be thinking about the presentation you have to give tomorrow or remember the email you forgot to send. Then you wonder if you locked the back door. Then it's back to the presentation, imagining everything that could go wrong. Your body is ready for sleep, but your mind won't stop.

This is one of the most frustrating aspects of insomnia. You can master all the physical relaxation techniques in the world, but if your mind is racing with worries, plans, and what-ifs, sleep remains elusive. Your body says "rest," but your mind says "think about everything right now."

The good news is that racing thoughts are not random or uncontrollable. They follow predictable patterns, and there are specific cognitive techniques that can interrupt those patterns. The following three evidence-based strategies for managing pre-sleep cognitive arousal - the worry dump, imagery distraction, and cognitive reframing - each takes 5 to 10 minutes and can be practiced as part of your wind-down routine or when you're already in bed.

Before we take a look at the techniques, let's understand why your mind races at bedtime and why this prevents sleep.

PRE-SLEEP COGNITIVE AROUSAL

Researchers use the term "pre-sleep cognitive arousal" to describe the mental activity that interferes with sleep onset. This includes worry about the future, rumination about the past, planning, problem-solving, and general mental chatter. Studies have consistently found that pre-sleep cognitive arousal is one of the strongest predictors of difficulty falling asleep.

Why does your mind race specifically at bedtime? During the day, you're distracted by activities, conversations, work, and external stimuli. Your worries and unfinished thoughts are pushed to the background. But when you lie down in a quiet, dark room with nothing to do, those thoughts rush to the foreground. Your mind finally has space to process everything you've been ignoring all day.

There's also an evolutionary component. Our ancestors needed to review the day's events and plan for tomorrow's challenges to survive. This mental review process would naturally happen during quiet, safe times, like lying in a shelter at night. The problem is that modern life generates far more worries and unfinished tasks than our ancestors ever faced, and our brains haven't adapted to turn off this review process when it interferes with sleep.

THE WORRY-SLEEP VICIOUS CYCLE

Research examining the daily relationship between worry and sleep has found a bidirectional pattern. Worry during the day and before bed predicts poor sleep that night. Poor sleep then predicts more worry the next day. This creates a vicious cycle where worry disrupts sleep, and disrupted sleep increases worry.

The content of pre-sleep worry often focuses on sleep itself. People with insomnia worry about not falling asleep, about how tired they'll be tomorrow, about the consequences of poor sleep. This creates what researchers call "sleep-related performance anxiety," which activates the sympathetic nervous system (the stress response) at exactly the wrong time. As we have learned, you can't sleep when your stress response is activated.

Why Trying to Suppress Thoughts Backfires

Many people try to deal with racing thoughts by telling themselves "stop thinking about that" or "just clear your mind." Unfortunately, research on thought suppression has shown that this can backfire. When you try not to think about something, you actually think about it more.

This is called the "rebound effect" or "ironic process theory." The part of your brain that's trying not to think about something needs to monitor whether you're thinking about it, which means it keeps the thought active in your awareness. It's like telling yourself "don't think about a pink elephant." The instruction itself makes you think about a pink elephant.

This is why the cognitive techniques in this chapter don't involve suppression. Instead, they work by redirecting attention, externalizing thoughts, or changing your relationship with thoughts. These work with your brain's natural processes instead of against them.

TECHNIQUE 1: THE WORRY DUMP (EXTERNALIZING THOUGHTS)

The worry dump is exactly what it sounds like: you write down all your worries, concerns, and unfinished thoughts before bed, getting them out of your head and onto paper. This simple technique has strong research support.

A study published in the Journal of Experimental Psychology examined the effects of bedtime writing on sleep onset. Researchers compared two groups: one group wrote a to-do list of tasks they needed to complete in the coming days, and another group wrote about tasks they had already completed. The to-do list group fell asleep significantly faster, an average of 9 minutes sooner than the completed tasks group.

The researchers concluded that writing about future tasks "offloads" those concerns from working memory, reducing cognitive load and pre-sleep worry. Your brain can stop trying to remember everything because it's now written down in a reliable external system.

Other studies have found that expressive writing about worries and concerns reduces rumination, decreases physiological arousal, and improves sleep quality - but, to work, the writing must be done before getting into bed, not while lying in bed trying to sleep!

How to Do a Worry Dump

Timing: Do this 30 to 60 minutes before bed, as part of your wind-down routine. It should come before your physical relaxation techniques (breathing, body scan, or PMR), not after.

Materials: Use paper and pen, not a phone or computer. The physical act of writing is important, and screens emit blue light that can interfere with melatonin production. Keep a dedicated notebook next to your bed for this purpose.

Duration: Set a timer for 10 minutes. This creates a boundary so the worry dump doesn't turn into an extended worry session.

The Process:

Step 1: Brain dump (5 minutes)

Write down everything that's on your mind. Don't filter, don't organize, don't judge. Just get it all out. Include:

- Worries about tomorrow or the future
- Things you need to remember to do
- Unfinished tasks from today
- Concerns about relationships, work, health, finances
- Random thoughts that keep popping up
- Things you're frustrated or angry about
- Decisions you need to make

Write in whatever format works for you: lists, sentences, fragments, whatever. The goal is to externalize the thoughts, not to create a polished document.

Step 2: Categorize if helpful (2 minutes)

Some people find it helpful to add a simple category next to each item:

- A = Action needed (something you can do)
- W = Waiting (something you can't control right now)
- N = Not important (something that doesn't actually need attention)

This helps you see that many worries are either not actionable right now or not actually important. You don't have to do this step if it feels like extra work.

Step 3: Schedule action time (2 minutes)

For items marked "A" (action needed), write a brief note about when you'll address them. This doesn't have to be detailed. Just:

- "Deal with this tomorrow morning"
- "Add to weekend to-do list"
- "Schedule time for this on Thursday"

This means that your brain knows there's a plan, and once there's a plan, it can stop trying to hold onto the worry.

Step 4: Close the notebook (1 minute)

Literally close the notebook and put it aside. You might say to yourself, "I've written it down. I don't need to think about this right now. I'll deal with it at the scheduled time."

This is a symbolic gesture that signals to your brain: the worry session is over.

Do's and Don'ts

Don't try to solve problems: This is not problem-solving time. You're not trying to figure out solutions. You're just acknowledging what's on your mind and creating a plan to address it later.

Don't judge your worries: Some worries will seem silly when you write them down. That's okay. Write them anyway. The goal is to get them out of your head, not to judge if they're "worthy" of worry.

Don't read it before bed: Once you've done the worry dump, don't read back through it. That just puts the worries back in your head. Close the notebook and move on to your physical relaxation technique.

Do it even if you don't think you're worried: Sometimes we're not consciously aware of the mental load we're carrying. Do the work anyway. You might be surprised what comes out.

What to Expect

First few times: You might write for the full 10 minutes and still feel like there's more. That's normal. You're clearing out accumulated mental clutter. Keep the 10-minute boundary anyway.

After a week: The time will become shorter. You're not accumulating as much mental clutter because you're clearing it daily. Some nights you might only write for 3 to 5 minutes.

Long term: The activity becomes a reliable tool for managing cognitive load. Your brain learns that worries will be addressed at the scheduled time, so it doesn't need to keep reminding you about them at bedtime.

Technique 2: Imagery Distraction (Redirecting Attention)

While the worry dump works by externalizing thoughts, imagery distraction works by redirecting your attention to something engaging but calming. You deliberately occupy your mind with detailed sensory imagery, leaving no mental space for worries.

And there is research that supports this. Work comparing different pre-sleep cognitive strategies found that imagery distraction was more effective than general distraction or thought suppression for reducing the time it takes to fall asleep. In other words, the imagery must be engaging enough to hold your attention but calming enough not to be arousing.

A study examining imagery distraction for insomnia found that participants who used this technique reported reduced pre-sleep worry, lower arousal, and improved sleep quality. The researchers noted that imagery distraction works because it occupies working memory capacity, preventing worries from entering awareness.

The technique is similar to "counting sheep," but much more effective because it's more engaging. Counting sheep is too simple and boring to hold your attention, so your mind wanders back to worries. Detailed sensory imagery is complex enough to keep your mind occupied.

How to Do Imagery Distraction

Timing: Use this technique when you're already in bed, after your physical relaxation technique. It's the last thing you do before sleep.

Duration: There's no set time limit. You continue the imagery until you fall asleep.

The Process:

Step 1: Choose your scene

Select a place that is:

- Familiar to you (somewhere you've actually been)
- Pleasant and calming (not exciting or stressful)
- Rich in sensory details (lots to notice and explore)

Good examples:

- A beach you've visited
- A favorite hiking trail
- A peaceful garden
- A cozy cabin
- Your grandmother's kitchen
- A quiet library

Avoid:

- Exciting or adventurous scenes (skydiving, theme parks)
- Scenes involving other people (too much social complexity)
- Scenes with tasks or goals (you're not trying to accomplish anything)

Step 2: Enter the scene

Close your eyes and imagine yourself in this place. Don't rush. Take your time to really arrive there mentally.

Where are you standing or sitting? What's the first thing you notice?

Step 3: Engage all your senses systematically

This is the key to making imagery distraction work. You're going to notice details using all five senses, slowly and deliberately.

Visual details: What do you see? Colors, shapes, light and shadow, near and far objects. Be specific. If you're at a beach, don't just think "blue water." Notice the exact shade of blue, the way the light reflects off the surface, the white foam of the waves, the texture of the sand.

Auditory details: What do you hear? Background sounds, subtle noises, rhythmic sounds. At the beach, you might hear waves crashing, seagulls calling, wind rustling through beach grass, the distant sound of children playing.

Tactile details: What do you feel on your skin? Temperature, texture, movement of air. Feel the warmth of the sun, the coolness of the breeze, the texture of sand between your toes, the smooth surface of a rock you're sitting on.

Olfactory details: What do you smell? Be specific. At the beach, you might smell salt air, sunscreen, the earthy smell of seaweed, the scent of pine trees nearby.

Gustatory details: What do you taste? This might be subtle. Maybe the salt on your lips from the ocean spray, or the taste of a drink you're imagining having.

Step 4: Move through the scene slowly

Once you've engaged all your senses from one vantage point, you can slowly move through the scene. Walk down the beach. Sit on a different rock. Wade into the water. Each time you move, notice new details with all your senses.

Don't forget to move slowly and notice everything. You're not trying to get anywhere or do anything. You're just exploring the sensory richness of this place.

Step 5: Return if your mind wanders

When you notice your mind has wandered to worries or other

thoughts (and it will), gently return to the imagery. Go back to the last detail you remember and continue from there.

Don't judge yourself for wandering. Just return. Each return strengthens your attention control.

Don't forget

Use the same scene every night: While you can change scenes if you want, using the same scene makes the technique more effective over time. Your brain learns to associate this particular imagery with sleep, creating a conditioned response.

Don't try to visualize perfectly: Some people are very visual and can create vivid mental images. Others are less visual and experience the scene more through other senses or just a general sense of being there. Both work fine. Don't worry if you can't "see" the scene clearly.

This is not goal-oriented: You're not trying to explore the whole beach or accomplish anything in the scene. You're just noticing details. If you fall asleep after noticing three things, that's perfect.

Boring is good: If the imagery starts to feel boring or repetitive, that's actually a sign it's working. Your mind is calming down. Keep going. Boredom is the gateway to sleep.

For the first few times your mind will wander frequently. You might feel frustrated that you can't maintain focus. That's normal. Keep returning to the imagery.

After a week you should be able to hold the imagery for longer periods before your mind wanders. You might even start falling asleep before you finish exploring the scene.

Technique 3: Cognitive Reframing (Changing Your Relationship with Thoughts)

While worry dump externalizes thoughts and imagery distraction redirects attention, cognitive reframing changes how you think about your thoughts. This technique comes directly from cognitive behavioral therapy for insomnia (CBT-I) and targets the unhelpful thought patterns that fuel anxiety and prevent sleep.

Cognitive therapy is based on the principle that it's not events themselves that cause distress, but rather our interpretation of events. Two people can experience the same situation (like lying awake at night) and have completely different emotional responses based on their thoughts about it.

Research on cognitive therapy for insomnia has found that changing dysfunctional beliefs about sleep significantly improves sleep outcomes. Common dysfunctional beliefs include catastrophizing about the consequences of poor sleep, unrealistic expectations about sleep needs, and misattributions about what causes sleep problems.

A study examining cognitive restructuring for insomnia found that participants who learned to identify and challenge unhelpful sleep thoughts experienced improvements in sleep quality and reductions in sleep-related anxiety. The technique is particularly effective for people whose insomnia is maintained by anxiety about sleep itself.

Common Unhelpful Thought Patterns

Before you can reframe thoughts, you need to recognize them. Here are the most common unhelpful thought patterns that interfere with sleep:

1. Catastrophizing: "If I don't sleep well tonight, tomorrow will be a disaster. I won't be able to function. I'll mess up everything."
2. All-or-nothing thinking: "I need 8 hours of sleep or the night is ruined. If I don't fall asleep in the next 10 minutes, I might as well give up."
3. Overgeneralization: "I never sleep well. I always have insomnia. This will never get better."
4. Mind reading: "Everyone can tell I didn't sleep well. They're all judging me. They think I can't handle my job."
5. Fortune telling: "I know I won't be able to sleep tonight. I can already tell this is going to be a bad night."
6. Personalization: "My sleep problems are my fault. If I were stronger or better at relaxing, I wouldn't have this problem."

Do any of these sound familiar? Most people with sleep difficulties engage in at least some of these thought patterns without realizing it.

How to Do Cognitive Reframing

Timing: You can do cognitive reframing in two ways. First, as a proactive exercise during your wind-down routine (before getting into bed). Second, as a reactive tool when you notice unhelpful thoughts arising while you're trying to sleep.

Duration: As a proactive exercise, this takes about 5 to 10 minutes. As a reactive tool, it takes just a minute or two per thought.

The Process

Step 1: Catch the thought

Notice when you're having an unhelpful thought about sleep. This requires awareness. Many unhelpful thoughts are automatic and happen so quickly we don't consciously notice them.

Common triggers:

- Looking at the clock
- Noticing you're still awake
- Thinking about tomorrow
- Feeling tired but not sleepy

Example thought:

"I'm never going to fall asleep. Tomorrow is going to be terrible."

Step 2: Identify the thinking error

What type of unhelpful thinking is this? Is it catastrophizing? Overgeneralization? Fortune telling? All-or-nothing thinking?

In the example above, it's a combination of overgeneralization ("never") and catastrophizing ("terrible").

Step 3: Challenge the thought with evidence

Ask yourself:

- Is this thought based on facts or feelings?
- What evidence supports this thought?
- What evidence contradicts this thought?
- Am I confusing a thought with a fact?
- What would I tell a friend who had this thought?

For the example thought:

- Evidence supporting: "I feel wide awake right now."
- Evidence contradicting: "I've felt wide awake before and still fallen asleep. I've had poor sleep before and still functioned okay the next day. Even if I sleep poorly, I can manage."

Step 4: Create a balanced reframe

Replace the unhelpful thought with a more balanced, realistic thought. The reframe should be:

- Honest (not fake positivity)
- Specific (not vague reassurance)
- Helpful (reduces anxiety rather than increases it)

Reframe for the example:

"I'm awake right now, and that's uncomfortable, but I've fallen asleep from this state before. Even if I don't sleep great tonight, I'll be able to get through tomorrow. One night of poor sleep is not a catastrophe."

Step 5: Let it go

Once you've reframed the thought, let it go. Don't keep analyzing it. Return to your imagery distraction or physical relaxation technique.

COMMON UNHELPFUL THOUGHTS AND HELPFUL REFRAMES

Here's a table of common sleep-related thoughts and more balanced alternatives:

Unhelpful Thought	Thinking Error	Balanced Reframe
"I need exactly 8 hours or I'll be exhausted."	All-or-nothing	"Sleep needs vary. Even 6 to 7 hours will allow me to function. Quality matters more than hitting a specific number."
"I'll never get better at sleeping."	Overgeneralization	"I'm learning new skills. Change takes time. I've improved at other things before."
"Everyone will notice I'm tired and think I'm incompetent."	Mind reading	"Most people are focused on themselves, not analyzing my appearance. And being tired doesn't mean I'm incompetent."
"If I don't fall asleep in the next 15 minutes, the whole night is ruined."	All-or-nothing, fortune telling	"Sleep onset time varies. Even if it takes longer tonight, I can still get restful sleep. One slow start doesn't ruin the whole night."
"This is all my fault for being so anxious."	Personalization	"Insomnia is complex and has many causes. I'm doing my best to address it. Self-blame doesn't help."
"I can't function on this little sleep."	Catastrophizing	"I'm more resilient than I think. I've functioned on poor sleep before. It's uncomfortable but not impossible."

Proactive Cognitive Reframing Exercise

In addition to using cognitive reframing reactively when unhelpful thoughts arise, you can do a proactive exercise during your wind-down routine:

Step 1: Write down 3 to 5 common unhelpful thoughts you have about sleep.

Step 2: For each thought, identify the thinking error.

Step 3: Write a balanced reframe for each thought.

Step 4: Read through your reframes before bed. This primes your brain with more helpful thought patterns.

Over time, the balanced reframes become more automatic. You won't need to consciously go through the steps. Your brain will start generating more helpful thoughts on its own.

Don't forget that reframes must be believable so don't use fake positive affirmations that you don't actually believe. "I'm going to have perfect sleep tonight!" is not helpful if you don't believe it. Stick with realistic, balanced thoughts.

Also, this is not positive thinking. Cognitive reframing is not about forcing yourself to think positively. It's about thinking accurately. You're correcting thinking errors, not pretending everything is perfect.

And some nights will still be hard because cognitive reframing doesn't guarantee perfect sleep. But it can reduce the anxiety that makes sleep problems worse. You're only aiming to break the worry-sleep vicious cycle.

Combining the Three Techniques

You don't have to choose just one cognitive technique. In fact, they work well together:

Worry dump (30 to 60 minutes before bed): Externalize all your concerns and create a plan to address them later. This clears mental clutter.

Cognitive reframing (during wind-down or in bed): When unhelpful thoughts about sleep arise, challenge and reframe them. This reduces sleep-related anxiety.

Imagery distraction (in bed, ready to sleep): Redirect your attention to detailed sensory imagery. This occupies your mind so worries can't intrude.

This sequence addresses cognitive arousal from multiple angles: externalizing, reframing, and redirecting.

Signs of Progress

First week: The techniques will feel effortful and mechanical. You might not notice immediate improvements in sleep. You're learning new skills, and that takes practice.

Second week: The techniques start to feel more natural. You might notice that worry dump reduces the volume of racing thoughts. Imagery distraction holds your attention for longer periods. Cognitive reframing becomes easier.

Third to fourth week: You start to see improvements in sleep onset time and sleep quality. Your brain is learning new patterns. The techniques are becoming more automatic.

Long term: These cognitive techniques become reliable tools for managing racing thoughts. You might also notice that you have fewer racing thoughts overall because you're addressing them proactively rather than letting them accumulate.

KEY HIGHLIGHTS

Racing thoughts follow predictable patterns and can be managed with specific cognitive techniques.

Pre-sleep cognitive arousal is one of the strongest predictors of difficulty falling asleep. It includes worry, rumination, planning, and mental chatter.

Three evidence-based techniques:

1. Worry Dump: Write down all worries and concerns for 10 minutes, 30 to 60 minutes before bed. Externalize thoughts, categorize if helpful, schedule action time, then close the notebook.
2. Imagery Distraction: In bed, imagine a familiar, pleasant place in rich sensory detail. Engage all five senses slowly. Return gently when your mind wanders.
3. Cognitive Reframing: Identify unhelpful thought patterns (catastrophizing, all-or-nothing thinking, overgeneralization). Challenge with evidence. Create balanced, realistic reframes.

These techniques work together. The worry dump clears mental clutter, cognitive reframing reduces sleep anxiety and using imagery distraction occupies your mind.

Remember not to suppress thoughts because thought suppression backfires. Instead, externalize, redirect, or reframe.

Practice during the day when possible. Learning these techniques when you're calm makes them more effective when you're anxious at night.

Give it three to four weeks. Your brain needs time to learn new cognitive patterns.

In the next chapter, we'll move on from techniques you can use before bed to your sleep environment itself. While cognitive and physical relaxation techniques prepare your mind and body for sleep, your bedroom environment can either support or undermine those efforts. We'll cover the 10-minute sleep environment audit and practical, budget-friendly changes you can make.

Chapter 9

Your Sleep Environment (The 10-Minute Audit)

Now for this chapter, let's meet James who has mastered his wind-down routine. He does his worry dump, practices PMR, and uses imagery distraction. His mind and body are ready for sleep. But his bedroom is working against him. The streetlight outside shines through his thin curtains, casting shadows across the ceiling. His partner keeps the room at 74°F because she's always cold. The neighbor's dog barks intermittently. His mattress has a permanent dip in the middle. And his bedroom doubles as his home office, so his desk is covered with work papers that remind him of tomorrow's deadlines.

James is doing everything right with his sleep techniques, but his environment is undermining his efforts. No amount of relaxation practice can fully compensate for a bedroom that's too bright, too warm, too noisy, or too associated with stress and work.

In the following pages you'll learn how to conduct a 10-minute sleep environment audit and make practical, budget-friendly changes to optimize your bedroom for sleep. We'll cover the five key environmental factors: temperature, light, sound, comfort, and associations.

You don't need to spend hundreds of dollars or completely renovate your bedroom. Small, strategic changes can make a significant difference.

THE SCIENCE OF SLEEP ENVIRONMENT

Your sleep environment affects sleep through multiple pathways. Some effects are direct and physiological (like temperature affecting your body's ability to cool down for sleep). Others are psychological (like visual clutter creating mental stress). Understanding these mechanisms helps you prioritize which changes will have the biggest impact.

Why Environment Matters

Research examining sleep quality across different environments has consistently found that bedroom conditions significantly affect sleep onset time, sleep efficiency, and subjective sleep quality. A comprehensive review of environmental parameters for optimal sleep found that temperature, light, and noise are the three most critical factors.

The challenge is that modern bedrooms often fail to provide optimal conditions. We use bedrooms for multiple purposes (work, entertainment, storage), we live in environments with artificial light and noise, and we prioritize aesthetics over sleep-friendly design. Many people have never consciously evaluated whether their bedroom supports or hinders sleep.

THE 10-MINUTE SLEEP ENVIRONMENT AUDIT

Before making changes, you need to assess your current environment. This audit takes about 10 minutes and will help you identify the biggest opportunities for improvement.

Timing: Do this audit during the day, not at bedtime. You want to evaluate your bedroom objectively, not when you're tired and frustrated.

Materials: Bring a notebook or use your phone to take notes. You might also take photos to help you see your space from a fresh perspective.

The Audit Process

Walk into your bedroom as if you're seeing it for the first time. Imagine you're a sleep consultant evaluating this space for a client. What do you notice?

1. Temperature Check

Stand in your bedroom for a few minutes. How does the temperature feel?

- Is it warm, cool, or comfortable?
- Does the temperature vary in different parts of the room?
- What's your thermostat set to at night?
- Do you wake up sweating or shivering?

Optimal range: Research indicates the ideal bedroom temperature for sleep is between 60 to 68°F (15 to 19°C), with most people sleeping best around 65 to 68°F (18 to 20°C). A study examining sleep across millions of nights found that each 1°F increase above 70°F was associated with poorer sleep quality.

Your notes: Write down your current nighttime temperature and if it feels too warm, too cool, or about right.

2. Light Assessment

Look around the room during the day, then return at night (or close your eyes and imagine nighttime conditions).

Daytime questions:

- How much natural light enters during the day?
- Are there windows? What direction do they face?
- What window coverings do you have?

Nighttime questions:

- How dark is the room at night? (Or imagine: can you see your hand in front of your face?)
- Is there light from streetlights, neighboring buildings, or outdoor security lights?
- Are there electronic devices with lights (TV standby light, phone charger, alarm clock)?
- Does light from other rooms leak under the door?

Optimal condition: Research on light exposure and sleep has found that even small amounts of light during sleep can disrupt sleep architecture and affect health. One study found that sleeping with just a small amount of ambient light increased heart rate and blood sugar levels. The darker your bedroom, the better.

Your notes: Rate your bedroom darkness on a scale of 1 to 10 (1 = very bright, 10 = completely dark). Identify specific light sources.

3. Sound

Stand quietly in your bedroom for 2 to 3 minutes. What do you hear?

Daytime sounds:

- Traffic noise
- Neighbor activity
- Household sounds (appliances, other people)
- Natural sounds (birds, wind, rain)

Nighttime sounds (or imagine):

- Do the same sounds continue at night?
- Are there additional nighttime sounds (neighbors coming home late, nocturnal animals)?
- Does your partner snore?
- Do you hear your own thoughts too loudly in the silence?

Optimal condition: Research tells us that nighttime noise can fragment sleep structure, reduce deep sleep, and cause awakenings even when you don't consciously remember them. The World Health Organization recommends keeping bedroom noise below 30 decibels (roughly the sound of a whisper) for the best sleep environment.

Your notes: List all sound sources. Rate how much each one bothers you (not at all, somewhat, very much).

4. Comfort Review

Evaluate your bed and bedding:

Mattress:

- How old is it? (Most mattresses should be replaced every 7 to 10 years)
- Are there visible sags or lumps?
- Do you wake up with back or neck pain?
- Is it too firm or too soft for your preference?

Pillows:

- How old are they? (Should be replaced every 1 to 2 years)
- Do they provide adequate support?
- Do you wake up with neck pain or headaches?

Bedding:

- Are your sheets comfortable?
- Is your blanket the right weight for the season?
- Do you wake up too hot or too cold?

Optimal condition: There's no single "best" mattress or pillow for everyone, but research has found that medium-firm mattresses work well for most people, and pillows should maintain neutral spine alignment. All you are trying to do is ensure that your bed is at a comfort level that means you're not aware of it.

Your notes: Write down any comfort issues. Be specific (e.g., "wake up with stiff neck" rather than just "pillow bad").

5. Association Evaluation

Look around your bedroom. What activities do you do here besides sleep?

Is there a TV?

- Do you work in your bedroom (laptop, desk, work papers)?
- Do you eat meals here?
- Is there exercise equipment?
- Do you spend time on your phone in bed?
- Is there clutter or visual chaos?

Optimal condition: Sleep research based on stimulus control theory has found that the bedroom should be strongly associated with sleep (and sex) only. When you use your bedroom for work, entertainment, or other activities, your brain learns to associate the bedroom with wakefulness and arousal rather than sleep.

Your notes: List all non-sleep activities you do in your bedroom. Note any visual clutter or stressful items (piles of laundry, unpaid bills, work materials).

THE FIVE KEY ENVIRONMENTAL FACTORS

Now that you've completed your audit, let's address each environmental factor with practical, budget-friendly solutions.

Factor 1: Temperature (The Most Important Factor)

Temperature is arguably the most critical environmental factor for sleep. Your body needs to drop its core temperature by about 2 to 3°F to initiate and maintain sleep. This is why you naturally feel sleepy when you're slightly cool and why a too-warm room makes sleep difficult.

The Science: Research on temperature and sleep has found that thermoregulation during sleep is crucial for sleep quality. A study examining the temperature dependence of sleep found that temperatures outside the optimal range (60 to 68°F) significantly disrupted sleep architecture, particularly REM sleep.

Practical Solutions

Lower your thermostat: Set your bedroom temperature to 65 to 68°F (18 to 20°C) at night. If you share your bed with someone who prefers warmth, this is a common source of conflict. Compromise by keeping the room cooler and giving your partner an extra blanket or heated blanket on their side only.

Use a fan: A fan serves double duty: it cools the room and provides white noise (more on that in the sound section). A basic fan costs $20 to $40 and can make a significant difference.

Choose breathable bedding: Natural fibers like cotton, linen, or bamboo allow better airflow than synthetic materials. If you wake up sweating, your bedding might be trapping heat.

Take a warm bath or shower 60 to 90 minutes before bed: This seems counterintuitive, but it works. The warm water raises your body temperature temporarily. When you get out, your body temperature drops rapidly, which signals sleepiness. This technique is supported by research showing that passive body heating before bed improves sleep onset and quality.

Keep your hands and feet warm: While your core needs to cool, cold extremities can prevent sleep. Wear socks if your feet are cold, or use a hot water bottle. Research has found that warming the hands and feet dilates blood vessels, which helps your core temperature drop.

Factor 2: Light (The Circadian Disruptor)

Light is the most powerful signal for your circadian rhythm. As we learned in Chapter 3, light exposure tells your brain if it's day or night. Evening and nighttime light exposure suppresses melatonin production and shifts your circadian rhythm later, making it harder to fall asleep.

The Science: Research on light and sleep has found that even dim light during sleep can disrupt sleep architecture and affect metabolic health. A study found that sleeping with just 10 lux of light (roughly equivalent to a nightlight) increased heart rate during sleep and reduced heart rate variability, indicating increased stress on the cardiovascular system.

Practical Solutions

Blackout curtains or blinds: This is the single most effective light-blocking solution. Blackout curtains can reduce light by 95% or more. They cost $30 to $100 depending on size and quality.

DIY blackout option: If blackout curtains aren't in your budget, you can use black fabric, dark blankets, or even cardboard covered with dark fabric to block windows. It won't look beautiful, but it works.

Cover or remove electronic lights: Use black electrical tape to cover standby lights on TVs, chargers, and other devices. Or better yet, remove these devices from your bedroom entirely.

Use a sleep mask: If you can't control light sources (like if you share a room or work night shifts and need to sleep during the day), a comfortable sleep mask blocks light effectively.

Install a dimmer switch or use lamps: Overhead bright lights in the evening suppress melatonin. Use dim lamps with warm-colored bulbs (amber or red spectrum) in the hour before bed.

Turn your clock away from you: If you have a digital alarm clock with a bright display, turn it to face away from you or cover it. Clock-watching during the night increases anxiety and disrupts sleep.

Factor 3: Sound (The Sleep Fragmenter)

Noise during sleep can cause awakenings, shifts to lighter sleep stages, and reduced sleep quality, even when you don't consciously remember being disturbed. Research has found that nighttime noise increases stress hormones and can have long-term health effects.

The Science: A comprehensive review of environmental noise and sleep found that noise above 35 decibels can fragment sleep structure and reduce restorative deep sleep. Importantly, you don't have to consciously wake up for noise to affect your sleep. Your brain continues to process sounds during sleep, and sudden or irregular noises can shift you to lighter sleep stages without full awakening.

Practical Solutions

Earplugs: Simple foam earplugs can reduce noise by 20 to 30 decibels and cost just a few dollars. They take some getting used to, but many people find them highly effective. Look for soft, comfortable ones designed for sleeping.

White noise machine or app: White noise masks irregular sounds (like traffic, neighbors, or a snoring partner) by providing consistent background sound. Your brain adapts to the steady white noise and is less likely to be startled by sudden sounds. White noise machines cost $20 to $50, or you can use a free app on your phone (just put the phone on airplane mode and place it across the room, not next to your head).

Fan for white noise: As mentioned in the temperature section, a fan provides both cooling and white noise. This is a budget-friendly two-for-one solution.

Soundproofing: If you have significant noise issues, consider:

- Heavy curtains (help block sound as well as light)
- Rugs or carpets (absorb sound)
- Weather stripping under doors (blocks sound from other rooms)
- Acoustic panels (more expensive but effective for serious noise problems)

Embrace silence or sound based on preference: Some people sleep better in complete silence, while others find silence too quiet and prefer gentle background sound. Experiment to find what works for you.

Factor 4: Comfort (The Foundation)

While comfort seems obvious, many people tolerate uncomfortable beds and bedding without realizing how much it affects their sleep. You spend about one-third of your life in bed. It's worth investing in basic comfort.

The Science: Research tells us that medium-firm mattresses generally provide the best support for most people, reducing back pain and improving sleep quality. However, individual preferences vary, and the "best" mattress is the one that feels comfortable to you and maintains neutral spine alignment.

Practical Solutions

Evaluate your mattress age: If your mattress is more than 10 years old, it's likely lost significant support. Mattresses are expensive, but there are now budget-friendly options (foam mattresses in a box). If a new mattress isn't in your budget right now, add it to your savings goals.

Use a mattress topper: If your mattress is too firm or has minor issues, a 2 to 3 inch memory foam or latex topper can significantly improve comfort. This is much cheaper than a new mattress and can extend the life of your current one.

Replace your pillows: Pillows lose support over time. If your pillow is more than 2 years old or you wake up with neck pain, replace it. The right pillow also depends on your sleep position:

- Side sleepers: Firmer, thicker pillow to fill the space between shoulder and head
- Back sleepers: Medium thickness to support natural neck curve
- Stomach sleepers: Thin, soft pillow (or no pillow) to avoid neck strain

Choose appropriate bedding: Your sheets and blankets should match the season and your temperature preferences. In summer, use lightweight cotton or linen. In winter, add layers. Having the right bedding weight prevents waking up too hot or too cold.

Keep it clean: Wash your sheets weekly and pillowcases even more frequently. Clean bedding feels better and reduces allergens that can affect sleep quality.

Factor 5: Associations (The Psychological Factor)

Your brain learns associations through conditioning. If you consistently use your bedroom for work, worry, or entertainment, your brain associates the bedroom with those activities rather than sleep. This is why you might feel alert and awake as soon as you get into bed, even if you were tired moments before.

The Science: Stimulus control therapy, a core component of CBT-I, is based on the principle that the bedroom should be strongly associated with sleep. Research has found that people who use their bedrooms only for sleep (and sex) have better sleep quality than those who use bedrooms for multiple activities.

Practical Solutions

Remove work materials: If possible, don't work in your bedroom. If you must have a desk in your bedroom (due to space constraints), create a clear physical boundary. Use a room divider, curtain, or even just turn your desk chair to face away from the bed when you're done working. Cover your desk with a cloth at night so you can't see work materials.

Remove or cover the TV: If you have a TV in your bedroom, consider removing it. If that's not realistic, at least don't watch TV in bed. Watch from a chair, then get into bed only when you're ready to sleep. Cover the TV with a cloth when not in use so it's not a visual reminder of entertainment.

Minimize clutter: Visual clutter creates mental stress. Your bedroom should feel calm and peaceful, not chaotic. Spend 10 minutes clearing surfaces, putting away laundry, and removing items that don't belong in a sleep space.

Remove stress triggers: Don't keep unpaid bills, work deadlines, or other stressful items visible in your bedroom. If you did your worry dump (Chapter 8) in your bedroom, store that notebook in a drawer, not on your nightstand where you can see it.

Create a sleep-only zone: Train your brain that bed equals sleep. Don't read, work, eat, or use your phone in bed. The only exceptions are sleep and intimacy. If you want to read before sleep, sit in a chair, then get into bed when you're ready to sleep.

Make it pleasant: Your bedroom should be a place you want to be. This doesn't require expensive decor. Simple changes like fresh sheets, a plant, or a calming paint color can make the space feel more restful.

YOUR ACTION PLAN

You've completed your audit and learned about the five key factors. Now it's time to create your personalized action plan.

Step 1: Prioritize based on your audit

Look at your audit notes. Which factors are the biggest problems for you? Prioritize those. You don't have to fix everything at once.

For most people, the priority order is:

1. Temperature (biggest impact, often free to adjust)
2. Light (high impact, moderate cost)
3. Sound (varies by individual situation)
4. Associations (free but requires behavior change)
5. Comfort (important but often requires larger investment)

Step 2: Start with free or low-cost changes

- Make the changes that don't cost money first:
- Adjust thermostat
- Remove electronic devices from bedroom
- Clear clutter
- Stop working in bed
- Turn clock away from you

These changes can be implemented tonight.

Step 3: Invest in high-impact, affordable solutions

If you have a modest budget, prioritize:

- Blackout curtains or sleep mask (if light is an issue)
- Fan (if temperature or noise is an issue)
- Earplugs or white noise (if noise is an issue)

- New pillow (if comfort is an issue)

Step 4: Plan for larger investments

If you need a new mattress or significant soundproofing, add these to your savings goals. In the meantime, use temporary solutions like a mattress topper.

Step 5: Implement changes gradually

You don't have to change everything in one night. Make one or two changes, evaluate the impact for a few nights, then make additional changes. This helps you identify which changes make the biggest difference for you.

COMMON CHALLENGES AND SOLUTIONS

Challenge 1: "My partner affects my sleep"

Bed partner issues are one of the most common yet under-discussed sleep problems. Many people struggle to sleep well because of their partner's snoring, movement, schedule, or temperature preferences. This can create tension in the relationship because discussing it feels like criticism.

Let's address the most common partner-related sleep issues directly.

Snoring

Snoring especially when it can be loud enough to prevent sleep or cause frequent awakenings.

There is an important note here because, snoring, especially loud snoring with pauses or gasping, can indicate sleep apnea. This is a serious medical condition that affects your partner's health and your sleep. Encourage your partner to see a doctor or sleep specialist for evaluation. Sleep apnea is treatable, and treating it improves both of your sleep and your partner's long-term health.

In the meantime, white noise machines can help mask moderate snoring and earplugs can reduce the volume. Some people also find that having their partner sleep on their side (rather than back) reduces snoring.

Partner has different sleep schedule

One of you is an early bird, the other is a night owl. Or you work different shifts. This creates conflict when one person is trying to sleep while the other is active.

Solutions:

Go to bed at different times. There's no rule that couples must go to bed simultaneously. The night owl can do quiet activities in another room while the early bird sleeps.

- Use sleep masks and earplugs so the sleeping partner isn't disturbed by light and sound when the other comes to bed later.
- The person with the later schedule should be considerate: use dim lights, move quietly, prepare for bed before entering the bedroom.
- Wake up at different times if needed. The early riser can use a vibrating alarm or wake up naturally, then leave the bedroom quietly.

Partner moves a lot during sleep

Some people are restless sleepers. They toss, turn, kick, or thrash, disturbing their partner's sleep.

Solutions:

- Larger bed: If you're in a full or queen bed, upgrade to a king. More space means less disturbance.
- Separate blankets: Each person has their own blanket, reducing the pulling and tugging.
- Mattress with good motion isolation: Memory foam or latex mattresses transfer less motion than innerspring mattresses.
- Check for restless legs syndrome: If your partner's leg movements are frequent and seem involuntary, they should be evaluated for restless legs syndrome, which is treatable.

Partner has different temperature preferences

This is extremely common. One person is always cold, the other is always hot.

Solution: Keep the room cooler (better for sleep) and give the warmer-preferring partner an extra blanket, heated blanket, or warmer pajamas. Research supports that cooler is better for sleep quality, so this is a case where the cooler-preferring partner's preference aligns with sleep science. Separate blankets also help because each person can adjust their own covering.

When separate beds or bedrooms might be necessary

This is a sensitive topic, but it's important to address. Sleeping in separate beds or separate bedrooms does not mean your relationship is failing. Many happy couples sleep separately because they both sleep better that way.

Consider separate sleeping arrangements if:

- One partner has severe sleep apnea that's untreated or treatment isn't fully effective

- Work schedules are incompatible (night shift worker + day shift worker)
- One partner has a medical condition that severely disrupts sleep (chronic pain, restless legs, severe insomnia)
- You've tried other solutions and both people are consistently sleep-deprived
- The sleep deprivation is creating significant relationship conflict

How to discuss this

Frame it as a health issue, not a relationship issue. "I love you and I want us both to be healthy and well-rested. I think we'd both sleep better if we tried separate beds/rooms. Can we try it for two weeks and see if it helps?"

Many couples find that sleeping separately improves both their sleep and their relationship because they're less irritable and more patient with each other when well-rested.

The bottom line on partner issues: Your sleep health matters. Your partner's sleep health matters. If sleeping together means neither of you sleeps well, that's a problem worth solving. Have honest conversations, try the practical solutions above, and don't be afraid to consider separate sleeping arrangements if needed. Prioritizing sleep is prioritizing your health and your relationship.

Challenge 2: "I can't afford blackout curtains"

Solution: Use aluminum foil, cardboard covered with dark fabric, or dark blankets to block windows. It's not pretty, but it's effective and costs almost nothing. Or invest in a good sleep mask.

Challenge 3: "I need my phone for my alarm"

Solution: Buy a simple alarm clock and keep your phone out of the bedroom entirely. If you absolutely must keep your phone in the bedroom, place it across the room (not on your nightstand), turn it face down, and put it on Do Not Disturb mode.

Challenge 4: "I live in a studio apartment, so my bedroom is also my living room and office"

Solution: Create clear boundaries using furniture arrangement, room dividers, or curtains. Designate one area as your "sleep zone" and keep work and entertainment materials out of that zone. Use visual cues (like covering your desk at night) to signal the move from work space to sleep space.

Challenge 5: "I rent and can't make permanent changes"

Solution: Most of the solutions in this chapter are renter-friendly. Blackout curtains, fans, white noise machines, earplugs, and sleep masks are all portable. Focus on these solutions rather than permanent changes.

Challenge 6: "I work night shifts and have to sleep during the day"

Solution: Light control becomes even more critical for you. Invest in high-quality blackout curtains or a sleep mask. Use white noise to mask daytime sounds. Consider explaining your schedule to neighbors so they understand why you need quiet during the day.

What to Expect

Immediate effects: Some changes (like lowering the temperature or blocking light) can improve sleep the very first night. You might notice you fall asleep faster or wake up less during the night.

First week: As you implement multiple changes, you'll start to notice cumulative effects. Your bedroom begins to feel more like a sleep sanctuary and less like a multi-purpose room.

First month: Your brain strengthens the association between your bedroom and sleep. You might notice that simply entering your bedroom triggers feelings of sleepiness.

Long term: Your optimized sleep environment becomes the foundation that supports all the other techniques you've learned. The physical space works with your wind-down routine, relaxation techniques, and cognitive strategies to create comprehensive sleep support.

JAMES'S STORY

Remember James from the beginning of this chapter, whose bedroom was working against his sleep efforts? Here's what changed for him.

James started with the free changes. He lowered the thermostat to 66°F (his partner was skeptical but agreed to try it with an extra blanket on her side). He removed his laptop from the bedroom and covered his desk with a cloth each night. He turned his alarm clock to face away from him.

Next, he invested in blackout curtains. The difference was immediate and dramatic. The streetlight that had been casting shadows all night was completely blocked. His bedroom was finally dark.

For noise, he started using a white noise machine. It masked the neighbor's dog barking and created a consistent, soothing background sound.

Within two weeks, James noticed significant improvements. He was falling asleep faster and waking up less during the night. His bedroom finally felt like a place designed for sleep rather than a multi-purpose room that happened to have a bed in it.

Three months later, James has maintained these changes. His bedroom is cool, dark, quiet, and associated with sleep only. Combined with his wind-down routine and relaxation techniques, his sleep environment provides the foundation for consistently good sleep.

What You Need to Remember

Your sleep environment significantly affects sleep quality. Even perfect relaxation techniques can't fully compensate for a bedroom that's too bright, too warm, too noisy, or too associated with stress.

The 10-minute audit evaluates five key factors: temperature, light, sound, comfort, and associations.

Temperature is the most critical factor. Keep your bedroom between 60 to 68°F (15 to 19°C), ideally around 65 to 68°F (18 to 20°C). Your body needs to cool down to initiate sleep.

Darkness is essential. Even small amounts of light can disrupt sleep. Use blackout curtains, cover electronic lights, or wear a sleep mask.

Reduce noise below 35 decibels when possible. Use earplugs, white noise, or fans to mask irregular sounds.

Comfort matters. Replace old pillows and mattresses. Use appropriate bedding for the season.

Associations are psychological but powerful. Use your bedroom only for sleep. Remove work materials, minimize clutter, and create a calm environment.

Prioritize based on your audit. Start with free changes, then invest in high-impact, affordable solutions. You don't have to fix everything at once.

In the next chapter, we'll address a common and frustrating problem: waking up in the middle of the night and being unable to fall back asleep. While the techniques you've learned so far focus on falling asleep initially, Chapter 10 will give you specific strategies for those 3 AM awakenings.

Chapter 10

When You Wake Up at 3 AM

Many of us experience the dreaded 3 AM or 4 AM awakening. And in this chapter we'll be looking at the example of Betty who is wide awake at 3:17 AM. She's been asleep for about four hours, and her mind is racing "Why am I awake? I need to be asleep. I have that important meeting tomorrow. If I don't fall back asleep soon, I'll only get five hours total. I'm going to be exhausted." She lies there, trying to force herself back to sleep, getting more anxious with each passing minute. An hour later, she's still awake, now panicking about how little sleep she's getting.

This scenario is one of the most frustrating aspects of insomnia. You've done everything right - you fell asleep successfully using your wind-down routine and relaxation techniques. But now all those techniques that worked at bedtime don't seem to help at 3 AM.

Middle-of-night awakenings, technically called "sleep maintenance insomnia," are different from difficulty falling asleep initially and so they require different strategies.

This chapter looks at exactly what to do when you wake up at 3 AM (or any time during the night). You'll learn the critical decision point (stay in bed or get up?), specific techniques for falling back asleep, and how to reduce the anxiety that makes middle-of-night awakenings worse.

The Science of Middle-of-Night Awakenings

First, let's understand what's happening when you wake up during the night and why it's so difficult to fall back asleep.

Why We Wake Up During the Night

Brief awakenings during the night are completely normal. Sleep occurs in cycles of about 90 minutes, moving through light sleep, deep sleep, and REM sleep. Between cycles, you naturally come close to waking or briefly wake up. Good sleepers have these awakenings too, but they fall back asleep so quickly they don't remember them in the morning.

The problem occurs when a brief awakening turns into prolonged wakefulness. This happens for several reasons.

1. Circadian rhythm factors: Your circadian rhythm naturally has a weak point in the early morning hours (around 3 to 5 AM for most people). Your body temperature is at its lowest, and your sleep drive is weakening because you've already discharged some of your sleep pressure. This makes it easier to wake up and harder to fall back asleep during this window.

2. Stress and worry: When you wake up, your mind might immediately engage with worries or start problem-solving. This activates your sympathetic nervous system (the stress response), which is incompatible with sleep.

3. Performance anxiety about sleep: As soon as you realize you're awake, you might start worrying about being awake, calculating how much sleep you're losing, and trying to force yourself back to sleep. This creates the same performance anxiety we discussed in Chapter 2, which makes sleep even more elusive.

4. Conditioned arousal: If you've spent many nights lying awake in bed, your brain might have learned to associate the bed with wakefulness and frustration rather than sleep. This is the opposite of the stimulus control principle we discussed in Chapter 9.

Sleep Maintenance vs. Sleep Onset Insomnia

Sleep maintenance insomnia (difficulty staying asleep) is different from sleep onset insomnia (difficulty falling asleep initially) in several ways.

Sleep onset insomnia usually responds well to wind-down routines and relaxation techniques because you're transitioning from wakefulness to sleep in a predictable, controlled way.

Sleep maintenance insomnia is trickier because you're already in bed, already tried to sleep, and now you're awake when you "shouldn't" be. The techniques that work at bedtime don't always work at 3 AM because the context is different.

Research on sleep maintenance insomnia has found that it's often related to increased physiological arousal during sleep, worry and rumination, and poor stimulus control (spending too much time awake in bed, which weakens the bed-sleep association).

The good news is that specific strategies for middle-of-night awakenings are highly effective, especially if you know what to do in the moment and have a plan before it happens.

The Critical Decision Point: Stay or Get Up?

When you wake up in the middle of the night, the most important decision you'll make is whether to stay in bed or get up. This decision should be based on a simple guideline called the "15 to 20 minute rule."

The 15 to 20 Minute Rule

If you've been awake for 15 to 20 minutes and you're not falling back asleep, get out of bed.

This is one of the core principles of stimulus control therapy, which is highly effective for insomnia. The rule exists to prevent your brain from learning to associate the bed with wakefulness and frustration.

Why this matters: Every minute you spend lying in bed awake and frustrated, your brain is learning "bed equals wakefulness and frustration." Over time, this association becomes stronger, and the bed itself becomes a cue for arousal rather than sleep. By getting out of bed when you're not sleeping, you preserve the bed-sleep association.

How to judge 15 to 20 minutes: Don't watch the clock. Clock-watching increases anxiety. Instead, use your subjective sense of time. If it feels like you've been awake for a while, if you're feeling frustrated, or if your mind is racing, it's probably been 15 to 20 minutes. Get up.

What if you're not sure?: Err on the side of getting up. It's better to get up after 10 minutes than to lie in bed awake for an hour.

What to Do When You Get Up

When you get out of bed, the goal is to do something boring and non-stimulating in dim light until you feel sleepy again. Then you return to bed.

Go to another room if possible: Leave the bedroom. This reinforces that the bedroom is for sleep only. If you live in a studio or can't leave the bedroom, at least get out of bed and sit in a chair.

Keep lights very dim: Use minimal lighting. A small lamp with a low-wattage warm bulb, or even just ambient light from a nearby room. Bright light will suppress melatonin and make it harder to fall back asleep.

- Do something genuinely boring: This is not the time for engaging activities. Good options:
- Read something dull (not an exciting novel, but something dry like a textbook or manual)
- Do a simple, repetitive task (folding laundry, organizing a drawer)
- Listen to a boring podcast or audiobook
- Do gentle stretching
- Sit quietly and practice breathing exercises from Chapter 5

Avoid these activities:

- Checking email or social media (too stimulating, blue light from screens)
- Watching TV (too engaging, bright light)
- Eating a full meal (activates digestion)
- Doing work (creates stress and association with productivity)
- Anything exciting or emotionally engaging

Stay up until you feel sleepy: This might be 20 minutes, or it might be an hour but wait for genuine sleepiness (heavy eyes, yawning, difficulty keeping eyes open), not just tiredness or boredom.

Return to bed when sleepy: When you feel sleepy, go back to bed.

Use your relaxation techniques (breathing, body scan, or imagery distraction from previous chapters) to help you fall asleep.

Repeat if necessary: If you're still awake after another 15 to 20 minutes in bed, get up again. Some nights you might need to do this multiple times. That's okay. You're retraining your brain.

Techniques for Falling Back Asleep (If You Stay in Bed)

If you wake up and you're not sure if 15 to 20 minutes have passed, or if you want to try falling back asleep before getting up, here are specific techniques to use:

Technique 1: The Quick Body Scan

Use an abbreviated version of the body scan from Chapter 6. You don't need to go through every body part in detail. Instead:

1. Notice your feet. Are they relaxed? Let them become heavy.
2. Notice your legs. Let them sink into the mattress.
3. Notice your torso. Let your belly soften with each exhale.
4. Notice your shoulders. Let them drop away from your ears.
5. Notice your face. Let your jaw release, your eyes soften.
6. Notice your whole body. Heavy, relaxed, sinking into the bed.

This takes about 2 to 3 minutes and can help you fall back asleep if you're not too aroused.

Technique 2: Extended Exhale Breathing

Use the natural breathing with extended exhale from Chapter 5. This is gentler than 4-7-8 breathing or box breathing, which might be too activating in the middle of the night.

Breathe naturally, making your exhale noticeably longer than your inhale. Don't count if that feels too effortful. Just feel the rhythm: breathe in, breathe out slowly and completely. Continue for several minutes.

This activates your parasympathetic nervous system and can help you drift back to sleep.

Technique 3: Return to Your Imagery Scene

If you've been using imagery distraction (from Chapter 8) at bedtime, return to the same scene. Your brain has already learned to associate this imagery with sleep, so it can be particularly effective in the middle of the night.

Go back to your beach, hiking trail, or whatever scene you've been using. Notice the sensory details. Move through the scene slowly. Let your mind settle into the imagery.

Technique 4: The Acceptance Method

Sometimes the best strategy is to stop trying to sleep and instead focus on rest and acceptance. This is based on paradoxical intention, which we discussed in Chapter 2.

Say to yourself (silently): "I'm awake right now, and that's okay. I don't need to force sleep. Rest is valuable even without sleep. I'm lying here comfortably, breathing, resting. If sleep comes, fine. If not, I'm still resting."

This removes the performance pressure and often allows sleep to come naturally.

Technique 5: Cognitive Reframing for Middle-of-Night Thoughts

Thoughts at 3 AM are often catastrophic. Use the reframing techniques from Chapter 8. For example: "I'm only going to get 4 hours" becomes "I can function on less. One night isn't a catastrophe." Reframing reduces anxiety and helps you fall back asleep

SPECIAL CONSIDERATIONS FOR DIFFERENT TYPES OF AWAKENINGS

Not all middle-of-night awakenings are the same. Here are strategies for specific situations:

Waking from a Nightmare or Anxiety Dream

If you wake from a disturbing dream, your heart might be racing and you might feel anxious.

What to do:

1. Get out of bed. Don't try to fall back asleep immediately when you're physiologically aroused.
2. Do some gentle movement (walking, stretching) to discharge the adrenaline.
3. Practice 4-7-8 breathing or box breathing (from Chapter 5) to calm your nervous system. These are more activating than extended exhale breathing, but that's appropriate when you need to actively calm down.
4. Remind yourself it was just a dream. You're safe now.

5. Return to bed when your heart rate has normalized and you feel calmer.

Waking to Use the Bathroom

If you wake because you need to use the bathroom, this is a physiological awakening, not insomnia.

What to do:

1. Use the bathroom with minimal light (nightlight in the bathroom, not overhead lights).
2. Don't check your phone or clock.
3. Return to bed and use quick body scan or extended exhale breathing to fall back asleep.
4. If you're waking to use the bathroom multiple times per night, this might be a medical issue (nocturia). Discuss with your doctor, especially if you're over 60.

Waking from Physical Discomfort

If you wake because you're too hot, too cold, or in pain, address the physical issue first.

What to do:

1. Adjust your environment (remove a blanket if too hot, add one if too cold, adjust pillow if neck hurts).
2. If pain is significant, take appropriate pain medication.
3. Once you're comfortable, use relaxation techniques to fall back asleep.
4. If physical discomfort wakes you frequently, review Chapter 9 on sleep environment and consider if you need a new mattress, pillow, or different bedding.

Waking with Racing Thoughts About a Specific Problem

If you wake with your mind fixated on a particular problem or decision, your brain is trying to problem-solve when it should be sleeping.

What to do:

1. Get out of bed.
2. Write down the problem and any thoughts about it (similar to the worry dump from Chapter 8, but in the middle of the night).
3. Schedule a time tomorrow to think about this problem. Write it in your calendar or planner.
4. Tell yourself: "I've written it down. I have a plan to address it tomorrow. I don't need to think about it right now."
5. Return to bed and use imagery distraction to occupy your mind with something other than the problem.

Early Morning Awakening (Waking at 4 or 5 AM and Can't Fall Back Asleep)

If you consistently wake up 1 to 2 hours before you need to and can't fall back asleep, this might be a circadian rhythm issue or a sign of depression.

What to do:

1. Review your light exposure from Chapter 3. Are you getting bright light in the morning? This can shift your circadian rhythm even earlier.
2. Try getting bright light in the evening (7 to 9 PM) to shift your rhythm later. This is the opposite of the usual recommendation.

3. Avoid naps during the day, which can reduce sleep pressure at night.
4. If early morning awakening persists and is accompanied by low mood, talk to your doctor about depression screening.

What NOT to Do at 3 AM

Just as important as knowing what to do is knowing what not to do. These common responses to middle-of-night awakenings make the problem worse:

Don't watch the clock: Clock-watching increases anxiety and makes falling back asleep harder. Turn your clock away from you or cover it.

Don't calculate how much sleep you're losing: "I've been awake for 30 minutes, so now I'm only going to get 3.5 hours..." This catastrophizing increases stress and activates your sympathetic nervous system.

Don't grab your phone: The blue light suppresses melatonin, and whatever you look at (email, news, social media) is likely to be stimulating or stressful.

Don't try to force sleep: You can't make yourself fall asleep through willpower. Trying hard to sleep creates performance anxiety, which prevents sleep. Use the acceptance method instead.

Don't lie in bed awake for hours: This is the most important don't. If you've been awake for 15 to 20 minutes, get up. Lying in bed awake for extended periods weakens the bed-sleep association.

Don't catastrophize about tomorrow: Thoughts like "tomorrow will be a disaster" are rarely accurate and always unhelpful. Use cognitive reframing.

Don't have caffeine: Some people think a small amount of caffeine will help them stay awake until a more reasonable bedtime. This backfires. Even small amounts of caffeine can interfere with sleep for hours.

Building Your Middle-of-Night Toolkit

Before you have a middle-of-night awakening, prepare your toolkit so you know exactly what to do in the moment.

Physical Preparation

Set up a boring activity station: Choose a spot outside your bedroom (or a chair in your bedroom if you can't leave). Have boring reading material, a dim lamp, and perhaps some herbal tea ready.

Prepare your environment: Make sure you can navigate safely in the dark or with minimal light. A small nightlight in the hallway or bathroom can help.

Have a notebook ready: Keep a small notebook and pen in your boring activity station for writing down racing thoughts.

Mental Preparation

Decide your plan in advance: "If I wake up and I'm not falling back asleep after about 15 to 20 minutes, I will get up and go to the living room. I will read my boring book in dim light until I feel sleepy. Then I'll return to bed."

Having a plan reduces the decision-making burden at 3 AM when you're tired and frustrated.

Practice your reframes: Review the cognitive reframes in this chapter during the day. When you wake at night, you'll be more likely to remember them.

Remind yourself of the goal: The goal is not to fall back asleep immediately. The goal is to preserve the bed-sleep association and reduce anxiety. Sleep will come when you're ready.

Getting Better, Step by Step

First week: You might need to get up multiple times per night. This can feel frustrating, like you're sleeping even less than before. Stick with it. You're retraining your brain.

Second week: You'll probably notice that when you get up, you feel sleepy more quickly. Your brain is learning that getting up is temporary and you'll return to bed soon.

Third to fourth week: Middle-of-night awakenings might become less frequent. When they do occur, you'll fall back asleep more quickly, either while still in bed or after a brief time out of bed.

Long term: Many people find that middle-of-night awakenings decrease significantly or disappear entirely. When they do occur, you have a toolkit of strategies and don't panic.

Reducing the Frequency of Middle-of-Night Awakenings

While this chapter focuses on what to do when you wake up, you can also take steps to reduce how often you wake up in the first place.

Optimize your sleep environment (Chapter 9): Temperature, light, and noise control reduce awakenings.

Address daytime habits (Chapter 3): Morning light exposure, caffeine timing, and exercise all affect sleep continuity.

Manage stress and worry (Chapter 8): The worry dump and cognitive reframing reduce the mental arousal that causes awakenings.

Strengthen your wind-down routine (Chapter 4): A consistent routine helps you enter deeper sleep, which is less easily disrupted.

Consider sleep restriction: If you're waking up frequently and spending a lot of time awake in bed, you might benefit from sleep restriction therapy. This involves temporarily reducing the time you spend in bed to match the time you actually sleep, which increases sleep pressure and consolidates sleep. This is best done under the guidance of a sleep specialist or CBT-I therapist.

Rule out medical causes: Frequent awakenings can be caused by sleep apnea, restless legs syndrome, chronic pain, or other medical conditions. If you're waking up multiple times every night despite good sleep hygiene, talk to your doctor.

Putting It All Together

We're now back with Betty, our example for this chapter, waking at 3:17 AM and lying in bed anxious for an hour.

Betty learned the 15 to 20 minute rule and prepared her toolkit. She set up a reading spot in her living room with a dim lamp and a very boring book about the history of accounting (her partner's old textbook). She practiced her cognitive reframes during the day.

The first night she woke up, she tried the quick body scan and extended exhale breathing. After what felt like 20 minutes, she still wasn't falling back asleep. Following her plan, she got out of bed and went to the living room. She read about accounting principles for about 30 minutes, feeling her eyes get heavy. She returned to bed and fell asleep within 10 minutes.

The second night, she woke again. This time she got up after about 15 minutes. She read for 20 minutes, felt sleepy, and returned to bed.

By the end of the first week, Betty noticed a pattern. She was falling asleep more quickly after returning to bed and her brain was learning that getting up was temporary - and bed meant sleep.

By week four, she was waking up less frequently. When she did wake, she often fell back asleep using the quick body scan or extended exhale breathing without needing to get up.

Betty still occasionally wakes during the night, but it no longer causes panic. She has a plan. She knows what to do. And most importantly, she's broken the cycle of lying in bed awake and anxious, which was making the problem worse.

Don't Forget

Middle-of-night awakenings are different from difficulty falling asleep initially and require different strategies.

The 15 to 20 minute rule: If you've been awake for 15 to 20 minutes and you're not falling back asleep, get out of bed. This preserves the bed-sleep association.

What to do when you get up: Go to another room, keep lights very dim, do something genuinely boring, stay up until you feel sleepy, then return to bed.

Techniques to try while still in bed: Quick body scan, extended exhale breathing, return to imagery scene, acceptance method, cognitive reframing.

Special considerations: Different strategies for nightmares, bathroom trips, physical discomfort, racing thoughts about specific problems, and early morning awakening.

What NOT to do: Don't watch the clock, calculate sleep loss, grab your phone, try to force sleep, lie in bed awake for hours, catastrophize, or have caffeine.

Prepare your toolkit in advance: Set up a boring activity station, have a plan, practice reframes during the day.

Be patient: The first week might feel harder as you retrain your brain. Improvements typically appear in weeks 2 to 4.

Address underlying causes: Optimize environment, manage daytime habits and stress, strengthen wind-down routine, rule out medical issues.

In the next chapter, we'll bring everything together. You've learned the science of sleep, the anti-perfectionism mindset, daytime and nighttime habits, multiple relaxation techniques, cognitive strategies, environment optimization, and middle-of-night tools. Chapter 11 will help you build your personalized sleep system by choosing which techniques work best for you and creating a sustainable long-term plan.

Part 3: Building Your Personal Sleep System

Chapter 11

Building Your Personal Sleep System

You've made it through ten chapters and learned a comprehensive toolkit for better sleep. You understand the science behind sleep, the importance of anti-perfectionism, how daytime habits affect night-time sleep, how to create a wind-down routine, three different physical relaxation techniques, cognitive strategies for racing thoughts, how to optimize your sleep environment, and what to do when you wake up at 3 AM.

That's a lot of information. And if you're feeling a bit overwhelmed, wondering "How do I actually use all of this?", then don't worry because this is the challenge with any new routine. You have many the tools, but you need a system for using them effectively.

This chapter will help you build your personal sleep system. Not a generic plan that works for everyone, but a customized one that is based on your specific sleep challenges, lifestyle, preferences, and what actually works for you. We'll walk through a step-by-step process to create a sustainable system you can maintain long-term.

Why You Need a Personal System

Think about the difference between having a toolbox full of tools and knowing how to build something. The tools are necessary, but you also need a blueprint, a process, and an understanding of which tool to use when.

The same applies to sleep. You now have a toolbox full of techniques. But you need:

A clear understanding of your specific sleep challenges: Are you having trouble falling asleep initially, waking up in the middle of the night, or both? Is your main issue physical tension, racing thoughts, or environmental factors?

A prioritized plan: You can't do everything at once. Which techniques should you implement first? Which will have the biggest impact for your situation?

A sustainable routine: Your sleep system needs to fit into your real life. If it requires two hours of preparation every night, you won't maintain it.

Flexibility: Your sleep needs and challenges might change over time. Your system should be adaptable.

A way to track what works: Without some form of feedback, you won't know which techniques are actually helping and which aren't worth the effort.

This chapter will help you create all of this.

Step 1: Identify Your Primary Sleep Challenge

Different sleep problems require different solutions. Start by identifying your primary challenge.

THE FOUR MAIN SLEEP CHALLENGE CATEGORIES

Category 1: Sleep Onset Difficulty (Can't Fall Asleep Initially)

Characteristics:

- Takes more than 30 minutes to fall asleep most nights
- Mind is racing with thoughts, worries, or plans
- Body feels tense or restless
- Feel tired but can't seem to transition to sleep

Likely causes: High cognitive arousal (racing thoughts), physical tension, poor wind-down routine, environmental issues (too bright, too warm), or anxiety about sleep itself.

Priority techniques: Wind-down routine (Chapter 4), cognitive techniques for racing thoughts (Chapter 8), relaxation techniques (Chapters 5-7), sleep environment optimization (Chapter 9).

Category 2: Sleep Maintenance Difficulty (Wake Up During the Night)

Characteristics:

- Fall asleep relatively easily but wake up during the night
- Difficulty falling back asleep after waking
- Wake up multiple times per night
- Early morning awakening (waking 1-2 hours before alarm)

Likely causes: Weak stimulus control (bed associated with wakefulness), environmental disruptions (noise, temperature, light), stress and worry, possible medical issues (sleep apnea, restless legs).

Priority techniques: Stimulus control and 15-20 minute rule (Chapter 10), sleep environment optimization (Chapter 9), cognitive reframing for middle-of-night thoughts (Chapter 10), daytime habits to strengthen sleep (Chapter 3).

Category 3: Mixed Insomnia (Both Sleep Onset and Maintenance)

Characteristics:

- Difficulty falling asleep initially AND waking during the night
- Variable sleep patterns (some nights can't fall asleep, other nights wake up)
- Sleep feels broken and unrefreshing

Likely causes: Multiple factors including high overall arousal, poor sleep hygiene, environmental issues, chronic stress, or underlying medical conditions.

Priority techniques: Comprehensive plan starting with foundations (daytime habits Chapter 3, sleep environment Chapter 9), then wind-down routine (Chapter 4), then relaxation and cognitive techniques (Chapters 5-8), then middle-of-night strategies (Chapter 10).

Category 4: Sleep Anxiety (Fear of Not Sleeping)

Characteristics:

- Anxiety about bedtime starts hours before bed
- Worry about having any sleep well tonight
- Performance anxiety about sleep itself
- Might actually sleep better than you think (sleep state misperception)

Likely causes: Perfectionism about sleep, past experiences with insomnia creating conditioned anxiety, catastrophizing about consequences of poor sleep.

Priority techniques: Anti-perfectionism mindset (Chapter 2), cognitive reframing (Chapter 8), paradoxical intention (Chapter 2 and 10), worry dump (Chapter 8).

YOUR PRIMARY CHALLENGE

Take a moment to identify which category best describes your sleep challenge. You might have elements of more than one category, but which is the most prominent?

Write it down: "My primary sleep challenge is ________________."

This will guide your priorities as you build your system.

STEP 2: ASSESS YOUR CURRENT BASELINE

Before implementing changes, it's helpful to know your starting point. This allows you to track progress and identify what's working.

The Simple Sleep Log (Not Perfectionist Sleep Tracking)

Remember from Chapter 2 that we're not aiming for perfect sleep tracking. We're using the "good enough" approach. You don't need to track every detail or measure every sleep stage. You just need basic information.

Each morning, briefly note:

- Approximate time you got into bed
- Approximate time you fell asleep (your best guess)
- Number of times you remember waking during the night
- Approximate time you woke up for the day

- How you feel this morning (1-5 scale: 1 = terrible, 5 = great)
- Any relevant notes (e.g., "had caffeine at 4 PM", "stressful day", "used PMR technique")

That's it. This takes about 60 seconds each morning. Do this for one week before making any major changes. This is your baseline.

Important: Don't obsess over the numbers. Don't calculate exact sleep efficiency or total sleep time unless you find it helpful. The goal is to have a general sense of patterns, not to create more anxiety about sleep.

Step 3: Choose Your Core Techniques

You can't implement everything at once. Based on your primary sleep challenge, choose your core techniques. These are the practices you'll commit to doing consistently.

For Sleep Onset Difficulty

Core techniques (do these every night):

1. Wind-down routine (Chapter 4): Start 30-60 minutes before bed. Include:

- Worry dump (10 minutes)
- Dim lights and put away screens
- Gentle physical activity (stretching or slow walking)
- One relaxation technique (choose your favorite from Chapters 5-7)

2. One physical relaxation technique (Chapters 5-7): Choose the one that resonates most with you:

- Breathing techniques (Chapter 5): Best if you prefer something active and structured
- Body scan (Chapter 6): Best if you prefer passive awareness
- Progressive muscle relaxation (Chapter 7): Best if you carry physical tension

3. Imagery distraction in bed (Chapter 8): Use the same scene every night to create a conditioned response.

Optional additions (try if core techniques aren't enough):

- Cognitive reframing for sleep anxiety (Chapter 8)
- Sleep environment improvements (Chapter 9)
- Daytime light exposure and caffeine timing (Chapter 3)

For Sleep Maintenance Difficulty

Core techniques (do these every night):

1. Sleep environment optimization (Chapter 9): Focus especially on:

- Temperature (60-68°F)
- Complete darkness
- Noise reduction

2. Stimulus control (Chapter 10):

- Use bedroom only for sleep (and sex)
- Get out of bed if awake for 15-20 minutes
- Have boring activity station ready

3. Middle-of-night toolkit (Chapter 10):

- Quick body scan or extended exhale breathing
- Cognitive reframing for 3 AM thoughts

- Plan for getting up if needed

Optional additions:

- Daytime habits for stronger sleep pressure (Chapter 3)
- Wind-down routine to enter deeper initial sleep (Chapter 4)
- Worry dump to reduce middle-of-night rumination (Chapter 8)

For Mixed Insomnia

Core techniques (do these every night):

1. Comprehensive wind-down routine (Chapter 4): This is your foundation.
2. Sleep environment optimization (Chapter 9): Fix the basics first.
3. One relaxation technique (Chapters 5-7): Choose your favorite and use it consistently.
4. Stimulus control (Chapter 10): Strict adherence to 15-20 minute rule.

Optional additions (add one at a time):

- Daytime habits (Chapter 3)
- Cognitive techniques (Chapter 8)
- Different relaxation techniques for variety

For Sleep Anxiety

Core techniques (do these every night)

1. Anti-perfectionism practices (Chapter 2):

- Permission slip exercise
- "Good enough" sleep log (not detailed tracking)
- 80/20 rule mindset

2. Worry dump (Chapter 8): Externalize anxious thoughts before bed.

3. Cognitive reframing (Chapter 8): Challenge catastrophic thoughts about sleep.

4. Paradoxical intention (Chapter 2 and 10): Try to stay awake instead of forcing sleep.

Optional additions:

- Relaxation techniques (but don't turn them into another performance)
- Sleep environment improvements
- Imagery distraction

Write Down Your Core Techniques

Based on your primary sleep challenge, write down your 3-4 core techniques. These are your non-negotiables, the practices you'll do consistently.

Example: "My core techniques are: (1) 30-minute wind-down routine with worry dump, (2) 4-7-8 breathing in bed, (3) imagery distraction with beach scene, (4) get up if awake for 15-20 minutes."

Step 4: Create Your Daily Sleep Schedule

A consistent schedule is one of the most powerful tools for improving sleep. Your body's circadian rhythm thrives on predictability.

Your Wake Time (Most Important)

Choose a consistent wake time that you'll maintain 7 days per week, including weekends. This is more important than your bedtime.

Why? Because your wake time anchors your circadian rhythm. When you wake up at the same time every day, your body learns when to start building sleep pressure, when to release cortisol, when to suppress melatonin. This creates a predictable sleep-wake cycle.

How to choose your wake time:

- Consider your work or life obligations (when do you need to be up?)
- Choose a time you can maintain on weekends (within 30-60 minutes)
- Make it realistic (don't choose 5 AM if you're naturally a night owl)

Example: "My consistent wake time is 6:30 AM, 7 days per week."

Your Bedtime Window

Based on your wake time and your sleep need (most adults need 7-9 hours), calculate your bedtime window.

Example: If you wake at 6:30 AM and need about 8 hours of sleep, your bedtime window is 10:00-10:30 PM.

Important: This is a window, not a rigid time. Go to bed when you feel sleepy within this window. Don't go to bed just because it's 10:00 if you're not sleepy yet. That creates the same performance pressure we're trying to avoid.

Your Wind-Down Start Time

Work backwards from your bedtime window. If you need 30-60 minutes for your wind-down routine, when should you start?

Example: "I'll start my wind-down routine at 9:30 PM to be ready for bed by 10:00-10:30 PM."

Your Morning Light Exposure Time

From Chapter 3, you learned that morning light exposure is crucial. Schedule this within the first hour of waking.

Example: "I'll get 15-30 minutes of outdoor light exposure between 6:30-7:30 AM."

Your Caffeine Cutoff Time

From Chapter 3, remember that caffeine has a 5-6 hour half-life. Calculate your cutoff time.

Example: "If I want to be asleep by 10:30 PM, my last caffeine is at 2:00 PM (8.5 hours before bed)."

Write Down Your Schedule

Create a simple daily schedule:

Wake time: ________

Morning light exposure: ________

Last caffeine: ________

Wind-down start: ________

Bedtime window: ________

STEP 5: IMPLEMENT GRADUALLY (THE 4-WEEK PLAN)

Don't try to implement everything at once. Gradual implementation is more sustainable and helps you identify what's actually working.

Week 1: Foundations

Focus: Establish consistent schedule and optimize environment.

What to do:

- Wake up at your chosen time every day (even weekends)
- Get morning light exposure
- Respect caffeine cutoff time
- Make basic sleep environment improvements (temperature, darkness, noise)
- Continue your simple sleep log

What NOT to worry about yet: Perfect wind-down routine, relaxation techniques, middle-of-night strategies.

Goal: By the end of week 1, your schedule and environment are consistent.

Week 2: Wind-Down Routine

Focus: Establish your evening routine.

What to add:

- Start wind-down routine at your scheduled time
- Include worry dump (10 minutes)
- Dim lights and put away screens
- Do one relaxation technique (choose your favorite)

What to maintain: Everything from week 1.

Goal: By the end of week 2, your wind-down routine feels natural and automatic.

Week 3: Refinement and Cognitive Techniques

Focus: Add cognitive strategies and refine what's working.

What to add:

- Imagery distraction in bed (if not already doing it)
- Cognitive reframing when anxious thoughts arise
- Fine-tune your relaxation technique (try variations or a different technique if the first isn't working)

What to maintain: Schedule, environment, wind-down routine.

Goal: By the end of week 3, you have a complete bedtime system.

Week 4: Middle-of-Night Strategies

Focus: Address middle-of-night awakenings if they're still occurring.

What to add:

- Strict adherence to 15-20 minute rule
- Boring activity station ready
- Middle-of-night cognitive reframes

What to maintain: Everything from weeks 1-3.

Goal: By the end of week 4, you have a comprehensive system for both falling asleep and handling awakenings.

After Week 4: Evaluate and Adjust

Look at your sleep log from the past 4 weeks. Compare it to your baseline from before you started.

Questions to ask:

- Are you falling asleep more easily?
- Are you waking up less during the night?
- Do you feel more rested in the morning?
- Which techniques seem to help most?
- Which techniques aren't worth the effort?

Based on these answers, adjust your system. Keep what works, modify or drop what doesn't.

STEP 6: TROUBLESHOOTING COMMON CHALLENGES

Even with a good system, you'll encounter challenges. Here's how to handle common ones.

Challenge 1: "I'm too busy for a 30-60 minute wind-down routine"

Solution: Start with a 10-minute minimum routine. The core elements are:

- Put away screens (2 minutes)
- Quick worry dump (5 minutes)
- One breathing technique (3 minutes)

This is better than no routine. As your schedule allows, gradually extend it.

Challenge 2: "My schedule is irregular (shift work, travel, etc.)"

Solution: Maintain as much consistency as possible within your constraints.

- Keep wake time consistent on days you're on the same shift
- Use light exposure strategically (bright light when you need to be alert, darkness when you need to sleep)
- Prioritize sleep environment optimization (blackout curtains, white noise)
- Be extra diligent about caffeine timing

Challenge 3: "I tried everything for 4 weeks and nothing improved"

Solution: This might indicate:

- An underlying medical condition (sleep apnea, restless legs, chronic pain). See a doctor.
- Depression or anxiety disorder. Consider therapy or medication evaluation.
- Need for professional CBT-I (cognitive behavioral therapy for insomnia). Seek a sleep specialist.

Don't struggle alone if self-help methods aren't working.

Challenge 4: "I improved for a few weeks but now I'm back to poor sleep"

Solution: This is common and doesn't mean you've failed. Possible causes:

- Increased stress (work deadline, family issue, health concern)

- Lapse in routine (stopped doing wind-down, inconsistent schedule)
- New environmental factor (construction noise, heat wave, new medication)

Identify what changed and address it. Return to your core techniques. Review Chapter 2 on anti-perfectionism to avoid catastrophizing about the setback.

Challenge 5: "My partner's sleep habits interfere with mine"

Solution: Have an honest conversation about sleep needs. Possible compromises:

- Different bedtimes (partner goes to bed later, you go earlier)
- Separate blankets (for temperature preferences)
- White noise or earplugs (for snoring or different wake times)
- Separate bedrooms (if space allows and both agree)

Your sleep health is important. Don't sacrifice it to avoid a difficult conversation.

Challenge 6: "I feel like I'm doing everything right but still not sleeping perfectly"

Solution: Review Chapter 2 on anti-perfectionism. Remember:

- Good sleep doesn't mean perfect sleep every night
- The goal is better sleep, not flawless sleep
- Some night-to-night variation is normal
- You might be sleeping better than you think (sleep state misperception)

Focus on how you feel during the day, not just how you think you slept.

STEP 7: BUILD FLEXIBILITY INTO YOUR SYSTEM

Your sleep system should be sustainable long-term, which means it needs to accommodate real life.

The 80/20 Approach

From Chapter 2, remember the 80/20 rule: consistency 80% of the time produces most of the benefits. You don't need 100% adherence.

What this means in practice:

- If you maintain your schedule and routine 5-6 nights per week, that's excellent
- Occasional late nights (social events, travel) won't ruin your progress
- Missing a wind-down routine one night doesn't mean you've failed

The key: Return to your system after disruptions. Don't let one off night turn into a week of abandoned routines.

Seasonal Adjustments

Your sleep needs and challenges might change with seasons.

Summer: You might need:

- Earlier wind-down time (still light at 9 PM, harder to feel sleepy)
- Extra cooling measures (fan, lighter bedding)
- Blackout curtains (sunrise at 5 AM)

Winter: You might need:

- Light therapy box in morning (if you wake before sunrise)
- Extra warmth (but keep room cool, warm your body)
- Later wake time (if your schedule allows, align with natural light)

Adjust your system as needed rather than fighting against seasonal rhythms.

Life Stage Adjustments

Your sleep system might need to evolve as your life changes.

New parent: Focus on sleep environment and stimulus control. Accept that total sleep time will be reduced temporarily. Use relaxation techniques for the sleep you do get.

Menopause: Hot flashes and hormonal changes affect sleep. Prioritize temperature control, consider layered bedding, talk to doctor about hormone therapy if appropriate.

Retirement: Without work schedule constraints, you might be tempted to have irregular sleep times. Resist this. Maintain consistent wake time even if you have flexibility.

Aging: Review Chapter 1 on age-related sleep changes. Adjust expectations (more awakenings are normal), but maintain good sleep hygiene.

Step 8: Know When to Seek Professional Help

Self-help methods work for many people, but not everyone. You should seek professional help if:

You have symptoms of a sleep disorder:

- Loud snoring, gasping, or breathing pauses during sleep (possible sleep apnea)
- Uncomfortable sensations in legs with urge to move them (possible restless legs syndrome)
- Acting out dreams or unusual movements during sleep (possible REM behavior disorder)

Your insomnia is severe and persistent:

- Insomnia 3+ nights per week for 3+ months despite consistent use of these techniques
- Significant daytime impairment (can't function at work, dangerous drowsiness)
- Insomnia is affecting your mental health (depression, severe anxiety)

You have co-occurring conditions:

- Chronic pain that interferes with sleep
- Mental health conditions (depression, anxiety, PTSD)
- Medical conditions that affect sleep (heart disease, diabetes, neurological conditions)

Professional help options:

Sleep specialist: Medical doctor who specializes in sleep disorders. Can diagnose conditions like sleep apnea and prescribe appropriate treatment.

CBT-I therapist: Psychologist or therapist trained in cognitive behavioral therapy for insomnia. Provides structured, evidence-based treatment typically over 6-8 sessions.

Sleep clinic: Facility that can conduct sleep studies (polysomnography) to diagnose sleep disorders.

Primary care doctor: Good starting point for discussing sleep concerns, ruling out medical causes, and getting referrals to specialists.

Don't view seeking help as failure. Professional treatment is often more effective than self-help for severe or complex sleep problems.

Three Example Systems

To help you visualize what a complete personal sleep system looks like, here are three examples based on different primary challenges.

Example 1: Emma's System (Sleep Onset Difficulty)

Primary challenge: Takes 60-90 minutes to fall asleep, mind racing with work worries.

Core techniques:

1. Wind-down routine starting at 9:30 PM
2. Worry dump (10 minutes)
3. 4-7-8 breathing (5 minutes)
4. Imagery distraction (beach scene)

Schedule:

- Wake: 6:30 AM (every day)
- Morning light: 6:30-7:00 AM (walk around block)
- Last caffeine: 2:00 PM
- Wind-down start: 9:30 PM
- Bedtime window: 10:30-11:00 PM

Environment:

- Blackout curtains installed
- Temperature set to 66°F
- White noise machine
- Work laptop stays in living room

Results after 4 weeks: Falling asleep in 20-30 minutes most nights. Still has occasional difficult nights, but no longer panics about them.

Example 2: David's System (Sleep Maintenance Difficulty)

Primary challenge: Falls asleep easily but wakes at 3 AM and lies awake for 1-2 hours.

Core techniques:

1. Strict stimulus control (15-20 minute rule)
2. Boring activity station in living room
3. Quick body scan when waking
4. Cognitive reframing for 3 AM thoughts

Schedule:

- Wake: 6:00 AM (every day)
- Morning light: 6:00-6:30 AM (coffee on patio)
- Last caffeine: 1:00 PM
- Wind-down start: 9:30 PM
- Bedtime window: 10:00-10:30 PM

Environment:

- Temperature at 64°F (cooler than before)
- Blackout curtains
- Earplugs for neighbor noise
- Clock turned away from bed

Middle-of-night plan: If awake for ~15-20 minutes, get up, go to living room, read boring history book in dim light, return when sleepy.

Results after 4 weeks: Still wakes occasionally but falls back asleep in 10-20 minutes most times. When he does get up, he's back to sleep within 30 minutes.

Example 3: Lisa's System (Sleep Anxiety)

Primary challenge: Anxiety about sleep starts at dinner time, worries all evening about not sleeping.

Core techniques:

1. Anti-perfectionism practices (permission slip, 80/20 mindset)
2. Worry dump (includes sleep worries)
3. Cognitive reframing (challenging catastrophic thoughts)
4. Paradoxical intention (trying to stay awake)

Schedule:

- Wake: 7:00 AM (every day)
- Morning light: 7:00-7:30 AM
- Last caffeine: 2:00 PM
- Wind-down start: 10:00 PM
- Bedtime window: 10:30-11:00 PM

Mindset practices:

- Daily reminder: "Good enough sleep is enough"
- Simple sleep log (not detailed tracking)
- Weekly review of reframes

Results after 4 weeks: Anxiety about sleep has decreased significantly. Realized she was actually sleeping better than she thought (sleep state misperception). Some nights still difficult, but no longer catastrophizing.

Your Personal Sleep System Template

Now it's your turn. Use this template to create your personal sleep system.

My primary sleep challenge: ________________

My core techniques (3-4 techniques I'll do consistently):

1.

2.

3.

4.

My daily schedule:

Wake time: ________________

Morning light exposure: ________________

Last caffeine: ________________

Wind-down start time: ________________

Bedtime window: ________________

My sleep environment priorities (top 3 things to optimize):

1.

2.

3.

My 4-week implementation plan:

Week 1 focus: ________________

Week 2 focus: ________________

Week 3 focus: ________________

Week 4 focus: ________________

How I'll track progress: ________________

My plan for handling setbacks: ________________

What You Need to Remember

A personal sleep system is more effective than randomly trying techniques. It's customized to your specific challenges and sustainable for your lifestyle.

Identify your primary sleep challenge: Sleep onset difficulty, sleep maintenance difficulty, mixed insomnia, or sleep anxiety. This guides your priorities.

Choose 3-4 core techniques based on your challenge. These are your non-negotiables.

Create a consistent daily schedule: Wake time (most important), morning light, caffeine cutoff, wind-down start, bedtime window.

Implement gradually over 4 weeks: Week 1 (foundations), Week 2 (wind-down routine), Week 3 (cognitive techniques), Week 4 (middle-of-night strategies).

Build in flexibility: Use the 80/20 approach. Adjust for seasons and life stages. Return to your system after disruptions.

Track progress simply: Use "good enough" sleep log, not perfectionist tracking.

Troubleshoot common challenges: Too busy, irregular schedule, no improvement, setbacks, partner issues, perfectionism.

Know when to seek professional help: Sleep disorder symptoms, severe persistent insomnia, co-occurring conditions.

Your system should be sustainable long-term. If it's too complicated or time-consuming, simplify it.

In the final chapter, we'll discuss how to maintain your progress over the long term, handle inevitable setbacks without losing momentum, and continue improving your sleep for years to come.

Before we move on to the next chapter I want to mention a technique called "Sleep Restriction Therapy" that you should know about. It's more advanced and requires careful implementation, and for this reason, it should only be tried with support from a professional, but it's one of the most powerful components of CBT-I.

What is sleep restriction?

Sleep restriction involves temporarily limiting the amount of time you spend in bed to match the amount of time you're actually sleeping. This might sound counterintuitive (you're already not sleeping enough, why would you spend less time in bed?), but it works by consolidating your sleep.

Here's the logic: If you're spending 9 hours in bed but only sleeping 6 hours, you're training your brain to associate the bed with wakefulness. By restricting your time in bed to 6 hours (matching your actual sleep time), you increase sleep pressure and strengthen the association between bed and sleep. Once your sleep becomes more consolidated, you gradually increase your time in bed.

Sleep restriction works through several mechanisms:

Increases sleep pressure: By staying awake longer, you build up more adenosine (the sleep-promoting chemical from Chapter 1), creating stronger sleep drive.

Strengthens bed-sleep association: Less time in bed means less time lying awake, which breaks the conditioned association between bed and wakefulness.

Improves sleep efficiency: Sleep efficiency is the percentage of time in bed that you're actually asleep. Sleep restriction dramatically improves this metric.

Reduces performance anxiety: When you're genuinely exhausted from restricted sleep, you stop trying so hard to sleep. It just happens.

The basic protocol

This is a simplified version. Ideally, sleep restriction should be done with professional guidance.

Step 1: Calculate your average total sleep time. Use your sleep log from Step 2. If you're sleeping an average of 6 hours per night, that's your starting point.

Step 2: Set your time in bed window. Take your average sleep time and add 30 minutes. If you sleep 6 hours, your time in bed window is 6.5 hours. This is the only time you're allowed to be in bed (except for sex).

Step 3: Choose your wake time. Pick a consistent wake time you can maintain every day. This is non-negotiable.

Step 4: Calculate your bedtime. Work backwards from your wake time. If you wake at 7 AM and your window is 6.5 hours, you can't go to bed before 12:30 AM.

Step 5: Stick to the schedule strictly. No napping. No going to bed early even if you're tired. No sleeping in on weekends.

Step 6: Track your sleep efficiency. After a week, calculate: (total sleep time / time in bed) x 100. If your sleep efficiency is above 85-90%, you can add 15-30 minutes to your time in bed window.

Step 7: Gradually increase time in bed. As your sleep consolidates and efficiency improves, slowly expand your window until you're getting adequate sleep (usually 7-8 hours).

When NOT to use sleep restriction

Sleep restriction is not appropriate for everyone. Do not use this technique if you have:

- Bipolar disorder: Sleep deprivation can trigger manic episodes.
- Seizure disorder: Sleep deprivation can lower seizure threshold.
- Safety-sensitive occupation: If you drive for a living, operate heavy machinery, or have a job where sleepiness could be dangerous, don't deliberately restrict sleep without medical supervision.
- Severe medical conditions: Heart disease, uncontrolled diabetes, or other serious health conditions require medical clearance.
- History of falls: Older adults at risk for falls should not use sleep restriction without supervision.
- Pregnancy: Sleep restriction is not recommended during pregnancy.

Why professional guidance is recommended

Sleep restriction is powerful but challenging. The first week or two can be very difficult. You'll be tired, possibly irritable, and your daytime function may temporarily worsen before it improves. A CBT-I therapist can:

- Monitor your progress and adjust the protocol as needed
- Ensure you're implementing it correctly

- Provide support during the difficult initial phase
- Identify if you're one of the people who shouldn't use this technique
- Combine it appropriately with other CBT-I components

Should you try sleep restriction?

If you have severe, persistent insomnia that hasn't responded to the other techniques in this book after 4-6 weeks of consistent implementation, sleep restriction might be worth considering. However, I strongly recommend working with a CBT-I therapist rather than attempting it on your own.

Many people see significant improvement from the other techniques in this book (stimulus control, cognitive restructuring, relaxation techniques, sleep hygiene) without needing sleep restriction. Try those first.

If you do decide to try sleep restriction on your own, start with a mild restriction (only 30-60 minutes less than your current time in bed) rather than a severe restriction. Monitor your daytime function carefully. If you feel unsafe or your functioning is severely impaired, stop and consult a professional.

The bottom line: Sleep restriction is a powerful tool in the CBT-I toolkit, but it's advanced and requires careful implementation. For most readers, the other techniques in this book will be sufficient. If you need sleep restriction, consider working with a professional.

Let's now continue to the final chapter.

Chapter 12

Maintaining Progress

Improving sleep when you are motivated and focused on it is one thing. Maintaining those improvements six months from now, a year from now, or five years from now, when life gets busy and stressful and your wind-down routine starts to feel like one more thing on an already long list, is the longer work.

This chapter is about how to do that without turning sleep maintenance into another burden.

What The Long-Term Change Looks Like

It helps to know what to expect, because long-term improvement in sleep rarely looks like steady progress upward.

The more typical pattern is a period of noticeable improvement when you first implement your system, followed by a plateau where things are better but not perfect. Then something happens like a stressful period at work, an illness, a disrupted routine, a run of late nights, travel, pain, hormones, or simply life getting in the way. Sleep gets worse for a while. You notice it, return to what helps, and recover.

Each time you move through that cycle, you get a little better at it. You recognise what has happened sooner. You panic less. You return to what works more quickly.

Understanding this pattern is the key because it helps you avoid the two mistakes that most often derail people. The first is expecting that once sleep improves, it will stay improved without any attention. The second is catastrophising when a setback happens, concluding that you are back to square one, that nothing has worked, or that you have somehow lost everything you built.

None of that is true. Setbacks are a normal part of long-term change, not evidence that the whole thing has fallen apart.

The First Few Months

In the first few months, you are still actively thinking about your system. You are consciously doing your wind-down routine, using your relaxation techniques, noticing how you are sleeping, and working out which tools fit your life.

The habits are not automatic yet, and the main risk is inconsistency when the initial motivation wears off.

The most useful thing at this stage is to plan for the situations that tempt you to skip things. Not just, "I'll try to keep up my routine when I'm tired," but something more specific, for example:-

If it is late and I am tempted to skip my wind-down, I will do a ten-minute version rather than nothing.

If I wake in the night and start clock-watching, I will turn the clock away and use the 15 to 20 minute rule.

If I have a stressful day, I will do the worry dump before bed, even if I do nothing else.

Specific plans are easier to follow than vague intentions.

It also helps at this stage to track your consistency rather than your sleep. Put a checkmark on your calendar when you complete your wind-down routine. Aim for five or six nights a week. That is the 80/20 approach. You are building evidence that you can do this, which will be important when the results feel slow.

When the Habits Become Familiar

Later, once the habits feel more familiar, the risk is less about forgetting to do the routine and more about letting the helpful parts drift away.

It might mean that things are going well, so you start cutting corners. The bedtime gets later. The caffeine cutoff slips. The phone comes back into the bedroom. You stay in bed awake for longer than you meant to. None of this feels too bad at first, but over time your pattern starts to change.

The antidote is to identify your keystone habits - the two or three practices that everything else is built on.

For most people, these are a consistent wake time, some form of wind-down routine (even if it's short), morning light and the discipline to get out of bed if you have been awake for 15 or 20 minutes and are getting frustrated.

Keep these in place through busy periods and disruptions, and your sleep is much more likely to find its way back. A brief monthly check-in is usually enough and ask yourself the following:-

Am I still sleeping reasonably well?

Am I still keeping the habits that help me most?

Has anything changed that I need to adjust for?

This does not need to become another tracking project. It is just a way of catching drift before it becomes a bigger problem.

Over the Longer Term

Over the longer term, good sleep habits can become as ordinary as brushing your teeth. You do not think about them much. They are simply part of how you live.

The challenge then is handling bigger disruptions like illness, grief, a new job, a new baby, travel, a change in living situation, or a stressful period that knocks your normal routine sideways.

When that happens, do not try to fix everything at once. Go back to the foundations - your wake time, your morning light, your sleep environment, your basic wind-down routine, and the way you respond when you are awake in bed.

The habits usually come back faster than you expect, because they have not disappeared. They just need to be reactivated.

When Sleep Gets Worse Again

At some point, sleep will probably get worse again for a while. That does not mean you have failed. It means you are human.

The first step is to recognise it early. The signs will probably be familiar by now. For example taking longer to fall asleep, waking more often, feeling less rested, starting to dread bedtime again, or noticing that you have quietly stopped doing the things that were helping.

Catching a setback early means a smaller course correction. Waiting until you are exhausted and demoralised makes everything harder.

Next, look for the cause and setbacks usually have one. The most common are increased stress, a major life change, seasonal changes, hot nights, travel, illness, a flare-up of pain, a new medication, or simple behavioural drift where the routines that helped have gradually slipped.

Ask yourself what changed, and when did my sleep start getting worse?

Often the answer is more obvious once you look for it.

Then respond to the cause, not just the symptom. If the problem is temporary stress, lean more on the worry dump, cognitive reframing, and your wind-down routine. If it is behavioural drift, return to your keystone habits. If it is a major life change, adjust your system to fit the new circumstances rather than trying to force your old routine into a life that has changed. If it seems medical, or linked to medication, pain, breathing, restless legs, or another health issue, talk to your doctor rather than trying to solve it through sleep habits alone.

Also watch for the catastrophe spiral. When sleep gets worse, the old thoughts can return quickly. You might catch yourself thinking "I have lost all my progress", "Nothing works" or "I will never sleep well".

None of those thoughts are an accurate assessment. It is the anxiety response that makes sleep harder. You have learned how to challenge those thoughts. Use what you know.

A Simple Reset

When you need to reset, keep it simple for the first week.

- Keep the same wake time.
- Get morning light.

- Restart your wind-down routine, even if it is only ten minutes.
- Write down worries before bed instead of taking them into bed with you.
- Use the 15 to 20 minute rule if you are lying awake and getting frustrated.

Do that for a week before deciding anything has gone wrong.

If you have drifted further away from your system, use the four-week plan from Chapter 11 as a reset. Spend week one on schedule and environment, week two on your wind-down routine, week three on cognitive techniques, and week four on middle-of-night strategies.

Track your consistency rather than your sleep. Be patient with the process. Most of the time, returning to the basics is enough.

Adapting Your System Over Time

Your sleep system should not stay fixed forever. It should evolve as your life changes.

The core principles remain the same, but the specific techniques you rely on may change. Things you needed every night at the beginning may become occasional tools. New challenges, such as hormonal changes, ageing, a different work schedule, a new relationship, a different bedroom, or a change in health, may require adjustments.

This is normal. The system was always meant to serve your life, not the other way round.

What is worth protecting is the understanding you have built and what you know i.e. sleep is a biological process that works best when you create good conditions and then get out of your own way. Trying too hard makes it worse. Good enough sleep is genuinely good enough. Difficult nights are not disasters and do not require a dramatic response.

LOOKING BACK, LOOKING FORWARD

Think back to where you were when you started this book. Your relationship with sleep may have been quite different then. It may have been more anxious, more effortful, more defined by the fear of another bad night and the exhaustion of lying awake trying to force something that would not come.

The goal was never to sleep perfectly.

It was to sleep better most of the time, and to handle the nights when sleep does not come without the panic and spiralling that make everything worse.

If you have that now, or even if you can see it becoming possible, then you have done something genuinely worth doing.

The techniques here will keep working best when you return to them consistently. And on the nights when they do not seem to be working, the most useful thing you can do is still the thing this book has been saying from the beginning, stop trying so hard, and give your body the conditions it needs to sleep.

CHAPTER 13

CONCLUSION

Understanding sleep and actually changing your relationship with it are two different things, and the second one takes time.

What matters now is not how much you have absorbed, but what you do next. You do not need to implement everything at once, and you do not need to be perfect about any of it. Pick one or two things that felt relevant to your situation and start there. Morning light, a caffeine cutoff, ten minutes of breathing before bed. Any of these, done consistently, can begin to help. The rest can follow when you are ready.

There will still be difficult nights. This is not a book that promises otherwise, because that promise would be dishonest and you would know it. Sleep is influenced by stress, hormones, pain, noise, the argument you had at work, and the thing you are worried about but have not quite sorted out in your head yet. Some of those things are within your control and some are not, and learning to tell the difference is part of what this book is really about.

The techniques here work best when you stop using them as a way to force sleep and start using them as a way to create conditions where sleep becomes possible. That is a subtle change in attitude, but it changes everything in practice. You are not trying to achieve sleep. You are allowing it.

If you take one thing from this book, let it be that good enough sleep is genuinely good enough. Not as a consolation, but as a fact. The relentless pursuit of perfect sleep is often what keeps people awake, and releasing that pursuit, really releasing it, not just saying you have, is often when things start to improve.

You know more than you did. You have tools you did not have before. That is enough to start with.

Sleep well.

Leave A Review

If you enjoyed this book and found it useful it would be truly appreciated if you could leave a review.

Bibliography

Chapter 1

National Institute of General Medical Sciences. (n.d.). Circadian Rhythms. Retrieved from https://www.nigms.nih.gov/education/fact-sheets/Pages/circadian-rhythms.aspx

Li, J., Vitiello, M. V., & Gooneratne, N. S. (2017). Sleep in Normal Aging. Sleep Medicine Clinics, 13(1), 1-11. https://doi.org/10.1016/j.jsmc.2017.09.001

Duffy, J. F., & Czeisler, C. A. (2015). Aging and Circadian Rhythms. Sleep Medicine Clinics, 10(4), 423-434.

Global Wellness Institute. (2025, April 2). Sleep Initiative Trends for 2025. Retrieved from https://globalwellnessinstitute.org/global-wellness-institute-blog/2025/04/02/sleep-initiative-trends-for-2025/

Barion, A., & Zee, P. C. (2007). A Clinical Approach to Circadian Rhythm Sleep Disorders. Sleep Medicine, 8(6), 566-577.

Benson, H., Beary, J. F., & Carol, M. P. (1974). The Relaxation Response. Psychiatry, 37(1), 37-46.

Edinger, J. D., & Means, M. K. (2005). Cognitive-Behavioral Therapy for Primary Insomnia. Clinical Psychology Review, 25(5), 539-558.

Chapter 2

Thakral, M., Von Korff, M., McCurry, S. M., Morin, C. M., & Vitiello, M. V. (2019). Changes in Dysfunctional Beliefs About Sleep After Cognitive Behavioral Therapy for Insomnia: A Systematic Literature Review and Meta-Analysis. Sleep Medicine Reviews, 49, 101230.

Eidelman, P., Talbot, L., Ivers, H., Bélanger, L., Morin, C. M., & Harvey, A. G. (2016). Change in Dysfunctional Beliefs About Sleep in Behavior Therapy, Cognitive Therapy, and Cognitive-Behavioral Therapy for Insomnia. Behavior Therapy, 47(1), 102-115.

Saldaña, K. S., Ong, J. C., Perez, I., & Roth, T. (2023). Acceptance and Commitment Therapy as an Adjunct or Alternative to Cognitive Behavioral Therapy for Insomnia. Current Sleep Medicine Reports, 9(2), 108-116.

Jansson-Fröjmark, M., Alfonsson, S., Bohman, B., Rozental, A., Lundgren, T., & Boersma, K. (2022). Paradoxical Intention for Insomnia: A Systematic Review and Meta-Analysis. Journal of Sleep Research, 31(1), e13464.

Scullin, M. K., Krueger, M. L., Ballard, H. K., Pruett, N., & Bliwise, D. L. (2018). The Effects of Bedtime Writing on Difficulty Falling Asleep: A Polysomnographic

Study Comparing To-Do Lists and Completed Activity Lists. Journal of Experimental Psychology: General, 147(1), 139-146.

Morin, C. M., Vallières, A., & Ivers, H. (2007). Dysfunctional Beliefs and Attitudes About Sleep (DBAS): Validation of a Brief Version (DBAS-16). Sleep, 30(11), 1547-1554.

Chapter 3

Blume, C., Garbazza, C., & Spitschan, M. (2019). Effects of Light on Human Circadian Rhythms, Sleep and Mood. Somnologie, 23(3), 147-156.

Drake, C., Roehrs, T., Shambroom, J., & Roth, T. (2013). Caffeine Effects on Sleep Taken 0, 3, or 6 Hours Before Going to Bed. Journal of Clinical Sleep Medicine, 9(11), 1195-1200.

Gardiner, C., Weakley, J., Burke, L. M., Roach, G. D., Sargent, C., Maniar, N., Townshend, A., & Halson, S. L. (2023). The Effect of Caffeine on Subsequent Sleep: A Systematic Review and Meta-Analysis. Sleep Medicine Reviews, 69, 101764.

Chan, J. K., Trinder, J., Andrewes, H. E., Colrain, I. M., & Nicholas, C. L. (2013). The Acute Effects of Alcohol on Sleep Architecture in Late Adolescence. Alcoholism: Clinical and Experimental Research, 37(10), 1720-1728.

Gardiner, C., Weakley, J., Burke, L. M., Roach, G. D., Sargent, C., Maniar, N., Townshend, A., & Halson, S. L. (2025). The Effect of Alcohol on Subsequent Sleep in Healthy Adults: A Systematic Review and Meta-Analysis. Sleep Medicine Reviews, 79, 101990.

Wang, F., & Boros, S. (2021). The Effect of Physical Activity on Sleep Quality: A Systematic Review. European Journal of Physiotherapy, 23(1), 11-18.

Leota, J., Nash, M., Tran, J., Teo, W. P., Banati, R., Barnett, M., Ciccone, N., Fazeli, W., Fripp, J., Domínguez D, J. F., & Drummond, S. P. A. (2025). Dose-Response Relationship Between Evening Exercise and Sleep in Healthy Adults: A Systematic Review and Meta-Analysis. Nature Communications, 16, 1166.

Godos, J., Grosso, G., Castellano, S., Galvano, F., Caraci, F., & Ferri, R. (2021). Association Between Diet and Sleep Quality: A Systematic Review. Sleep Medicine Reviews, 57, 101430.

St-Onge, M. P., Roberts, A., Shechter, A., & Choudhury, A. R. (2016). Fiber and Saturated Fat Are Associated with Sleep Arousals and Slow Wave Sleep. Journal of Clinical Sleep Medicine, 12(1), 19-24.

Chapter 4

Mindell, J. A., Li, A. M., Sadeh, A., Kwon, R., & Goh, D. Y. (2015). Bedtime Routines for Young Children: A Dose-Dependent Association with Sleep Outcomes. Sleep, 38(5), 717-722.

Larsen, K. L., Arendt, K., & Harmon, B. (2022). Factors Associated with Consistent Bedtime Routines and Their Relationship to Sleep Quality in College Students. Journal of American College Health, 70(8), 2344-2351.

Walker, J., Muench, A., Perlis, M. L., & Vargas, I. (2022). Cognitive Behavioral Therapy for Insomnia (CBT-I): A Primer. Sleep Medicine Clinics, 17(2), 85-106.

Bootzin, R. R., & Epstein, D. R. (2011). Stimulus Control. In M. Perlis, M. Aloia, & B. Kuhn (Eds.), Behavioral Treatments for Sleep Disorders (pp. 21-30). Academic Press.

Chang, A. M., Aeschbach, D., Duffy, J. F., & Czeisler, C. A. (2015). Evening Use of Light-Emitting eReaders Negatively Affects Sleep, Circadian Timing, and Next-Morning Alertness. Proceedings of the National Academy of Sciences, 112(4), 1232-1237.

Castro-Santos, L., Rodríguez-Fernández, J. E., Rodríguez-Fernández, M., Pinto-Fraga, J., & Blanco-Pintos, T. (2023). Sleep and Circadian Hygiene Practices Association with Sleep Quality: A Cross-Sectional Study. Sleep Epidemiology, 3, 100057.

Alanazi, E. M., Alanazi, A. R., Alqahtani, S. S., Alshehri, M. M., Alshehri, M. S., Alqahtani, M. M., & Alqahtani, A. A. (2023). Sleep Hygiene Practices and Its Impact on Mental Health and Functional Performance Among Adults in Tabuk City: A Cross-Sectional Study. Cureus, 15(2), e34501.

Vierra, J., Boonla, O., & Prasertsri, P. (2022). Effects of Sleep Deprivation and 4-7-8 Breathing Control on Heart Rate Variability, Blood Pressure, Blood Glucose, and Endothelial Function in Healthy Young Adults. Physiological Reports, 10(13), e15389.

Chapter 5

Vierra, J., Boonla, O., & Prasertsri, P. (2022). Effects of Sleep Deprivation and 4-7-8 Breathing Control on Heart Rate Variability, Blood Pressure, Blood Glucose, and Endothelial Function in Healthy Young Adults. Physiological Reports, 10(13), e15389.

Eskici İlgin, V., & Yayla, A. (2023). Effect of the 4-7-8 Breathing Technique on Pain Level and Sleep Quality of Patients After Laparoscopic Bariatric Surgery: A Randomized Controlled Study. Bariatric Surgical Practice and Patient Care, 18(2), 86-93.

Myerholtz, L. (2023). Take a Deep Breath. Family Medicine, 55(10), 695-697.

Ahmed, A., Devi, R. G., & Priya, A. J. (2021). Effect of Box Breathing Technique on Lung Function Test. Journal of Pharmaceutical Negative Results, 12(3), 1234-1239.

Laborde, S., Allen, M. S., Borges, U., Dosseville, F., Hosang, T. J., Iskra, M., Mosley, E., Salvotti, C., Spolverato, L., Zammit, N., & Javelle, F. (2022). Effects of Voluntary Slow Breathing on Heart Rate and Heart Rate Variability: A Systematic Review and a Meta-Analysis. Neuroscience & Biobehavioral Reviews, 138, 104711.

Russo, M. A., Santarelli, D. M., & O'Rourke, D. (2017). The Physiological Effects of Slow Breathing in the Healthy Human. Breathe, 13(4), 298-309.

.Zaccaro, A., Piarulli, A., Laurino, M., Garbella, E., Menicucci, D., Neri, B., & Gemignani, A. (2018). How Breath-Control Can Change Your Life: A Systematic

Review on Psycho-Physiological Correlates of Slow Breathing. Frontiers in Human Neuroscience, 12, 353.

Chapter 6

Rusch, H. L., Rosario, M., Levison, L. M., Olivera, A., Livingston, W. S., Wu, T., & Gill, J. M. (2019). The Effect of Mindfulness Meditation on Sleep Quality: A Systematic Review and Meta-Analysis of Randomized Controlled Trials. Annals of the New York Academy of Sciences, 1445(1), 5-16.

de Bruin, E. J., Meijer, A. M., & Bögels, S. M. (2020). The Contribution of a Body Scan Mindfulness Meditation to Effectiveness of Internet-Delivered CBT for Insomnia in Adolescents. Mindfulness, 11(4), 872-882.

Gan, R., Zhang, L., Chen, S., & Huang, H. (2022). The Effects of Body Scan Meditation: A Systematic Review and Meta-Analysis. Applied Psychology: Health and Well-Being, 14(4), 1202-1228.

Iliakis, I., Lam, J., Lyall, L. M., Schueller, S. M., & Torous, J. (2024). Assessing the Impact of the Mindfulness-Based Body Scan Meditation on Stress and Sleep: Ecological Momentary Assessment Study. JMIR Formative Research, 8, e55408.

Kabat-Zinn, J. (2013). Full Catastrophe Living: Using the Wisdom of Your Body and Mind to Face Stress, Pain, and Illness (Revised Edition). Bantam Books.

Ong, J. C., Manber, R., Segal, Z., Xia, Y., Shapiro, S., & Wyatt, J. K. (2014). A Randomized Controlled Trial of Mindfulness Meditation for Chronic Insomnia. Sleep, 37(9), 1553-1563.

Chapter 7

Toussaint, L., Nguyen, Q. A., Roettger, C., Dixon, K., Offenbächer, M., Kohls, N., Hirsch, J., & Sirois, F. (2021). Effectiveness of Progressive Muscle Relaxation, Deep Breathing, and Guided Imagery in Promoting Psychological and Physiological States of Relaxation. Evidence-Based Complementary and Alternative Medicine, 2021, 5924040.

Simon, K. C., & McDevitt, E. A. (2023). Progressive Muscle Relaxation Increases Slow-Wave Sleep During a Daytime Nap. Journal of Cognitive Enhancement, 7, 83-94.

Luo, Y., Zhang, X., Huang, W., Liu, Y., & Chen, X. (2024). Progressive Muscle Relaxation Alleviates Anxiety and Depression, and Improves Sleep Quality in Patients: A Systematic Review and Meta-Analysis. Frontiers in Psychology, 15, 1337318.

Kahreh, F. S., Abdi, A., Khatony, A., Salari, N., & Hosseinian-Far, M. (2024). The Effect of Jacobson Relaxation Technique on Sleep Quality of Patients With Cancer Under Chemotherapy: A Randomized Clinical Trial. SAGE Open Medicine, 12, 1-8.

Aksu, S. P., & Aksu, M. (2022). Effects of Health Education and Progressive Muscle Relaxation on Vasomotor Symptoms and Insomnia in Perimenopausal Women: A

Randomized Controlled Trial. Archives of Gynecology and Obstetrics, 306(5), 1711-1720.

Jacobson, E. (1938). Progressive Relaxation. University of Chicago Press.

Chapter 8

Scullin, M. K., Krueger, M. L., Ballard, H. K., Pruett, N., & Bliwise, D. L. (2018). The Effects of Bedtime Writing on Difficulty Falling Asleep: A Polysomnographic Study Comparing To-Do Lists and Completed Activity Lists. Journal of Experimental Psychology: General, 147(1), 139-146.

McGowan, S. K., Behar, E., & Luhmann, M. (2016). Examining the Relationship Between Worry and Sleep: A Daily Process Approach. Behavior Therapy, 47(4), 460-473.

Digdon, N., & Koble, A. (2011). Effects of Constructive Worry, Imagery Distraction, and Gratitude Interventions on Sleep Quality: A Pilot Trial. Applied Psychology: Health and Well-Being, 3(2), 193-206.

Harvey, A. G., & Payne, S. (2002). The Management of Unwanted Pre-Sleep Thoughts in Insomnia: Distraction with Imagery Versus General Distraction. Behaviour Research and Therapy, 40(3), 267-277.

Morin, C. M. (2010). Cognitive Therapy for Dysfunctional Beliefs About Sleep and Insomnia. In M. Perlis, M. Aloia, & B. Kuhn (Eds.), Behavioral Treatments for Sleep Disorders (pp. 67-75). Academic Press.

Brewer, J. A., Elwafi, H. M., & Davis, J. H. (2020). Can Mindfulness Mechanistically Target Worry to Improve Sleep? Theory and Study Protocol. Frontiers in Psychology, 11, 1699.

Wegner, D. M., Schneider, D. J., Carter, S. R., & White, T. L. (1987). Paradoxical Effects of Thought Suppression. Journal of Personality and Social Psychology, 53(1), 5-13.

Rossman, J. (2019). Cognitive-Behavioral Therapy for Insomnia: An Effective and Underutilized Treatment for Insomnia. American Journal of Lifestyle Medicine, 13(6), 544-547.

Chapter 9

Harding, E. C., Franks, N. P., & Wisden, W. (2019). The Temperature Dependence of Sleep. Frontiers in Neuroscience, 13, 336.

Chevance, G., Golaszewski, N. M., Tipton, M., Barger, L. K., & Czeisler, C. A. (2024). A Systematic Review of Ambient Heat and Sleep in a Warming Climate. Sleep Medicine Reviews, 74, 101897.

Mason, I. C., Grimaldi, D., Reid, K. J., Warlick, C. D., Malkani, R. G., Abbott, S. M., & Zee, P. C. (2022). Light Exposure During Sleep Impairs Cardiometabolic Function. Proceedings of the National Academy of Sciences, 119(12), e2113290119.

Sweeney, M. R., Nichols, H. B., Jones, R. R., Olshan, A. F., Keil, A. P., Engel, L. S., Sandler, D. P., & Jackson, C. L. (2024). Exposure to Indoor Light at Night in

Relation to Multiple Sleep Dimensions and Sleep Difficulties. Sleep, 47(2), zsad100.

Smith, M. G., Cordoza, M., & Basner, M. (2022). Environmental Noise and Effects on Sleep: An Update to the WHO Systematic Review and Meta-Analysis. Environmental Health Perspectives, 130(7), 076001.

Jacobson, B. H., Boolani, A., & Smith, D. B. (2009). Changes in Back Pain, Sleep Quality, and Perceived Stress After Introduction of New Bedding Systems. Journal of Chiropractic Medicine, 8(1), 1-8.

Bootzin, R. R., & Epstein, D. R. (2011). Stimulus Control. In M. Perlis, M. Aloia, & B. Kuhn (Eds.), Behavioral Treatments for Sleep Disorders (pp. 21-30). Academic Press.

Chapter 10

Fiorentino, L., & Martin, J. L. (2010). Awake at 4 A.M.: Treatment of Insomnia With Early Morning Awakenings Among Older Adults. Journal of Clinical Psychology, 66(11), 1161-1174.

Jansson-Fröjmark, M., Nordenstam, L., & Norell-Clarke, A. (2024). Stimulus Control for Insomnia: A Systematic Review and Meta-Analysis. Journal of Sleep Research, 33(3), e14002.

Verreault, M. D., Granger, E., Neveu, X., Turcotte, I., & Morin, C. M. (2024). The Effectiveness of Stimulus Control in Cognitive Behavioural Therapy for Insomnia in Adults: A Systematic Review and Network Meta-Analysis. Journal of Sleep Research, 33(3), e14008.

Perlis, M. L., Jungquist, C., Smith, M. T., & Posner, D. (2005). Cognitive Behavioral Treatment of Insomnia: A Session-by-Session Guide. Springer.

Morin, C. M., & Espie, C. A. (2003). Insomnia: A Clinical Guide to Assessment and Treatment. Springer.

Sateia, M. J., Buysse, D. J., Krystal, A. D., Neubauer, D. N., & Heald, J. L. (2017). Clinical Practice Guideline for the Pharmacologic Treatment of Chronic Insomnia in Adults: An American Academy of Sleep Medicine Clinical Practice Guideline. Journal of Clinical Sleep Medicine, 13(2), 307-349.

Matheson, E., & Hainer, B. L. (2017). Insomnia: Pharmacologic Therapy. American Family Physician, 96(1), 29-35.

Chapter 11

Edinger, J. D., & Carney, C. E. (2015). Overcoming Insomnia: A Cognitive-Behavioral Therapy Approach, Therapist Guide (2nd ed.). Oxford University Press.

Irish, L. A., Kline, C. E., Gunn, H. E., Buysse, D. J., & Hall, M. H. (2015). The Role of Sleep Hygiene in Promoting Public Health: A Review of Empirical Evidence. Sleep Medicine Reviews, 22, 23-36.

Manber, R., & Carney, C. E. (2015). Treatment Plans and Interventions for Insomnia: A Case Formulation Approach. Guilford Press.

www.ingramcontent.com/pod-product-compliance
Lightning Source LLC
LaVergne TN
LVHW040514210926
848480LV00005BA/1460
9781918808032